PUBLICATION
OF THE
**AMERICAN
DIALECT
SOCIETY**

NUMBER 79

**UNDER COVER OF LAW:
MORE ON THE LEGALITY
OF SURREPTITIOUS
RECORDING**

THOMAS E. MURRAY
with the assistance of
CARMIN D. ROSS-MURRAY

**PUBLISHED FOR
THE SOCIETY BY
THE UNIVERSITY
OF ALABAMA PRESS**
TUSCALOOSA AND LONDON

Copyright © 1996
American Dialect Society
ISBN: 0-8173-0825-3

Library of Congress Cataloging-in-Publication Data

Under cover of law : more on the legality of surreptitious recording /
   [edited by] Thomas E. Murray with the assistance of Carmin D.
   Ross-Murray
      p.   cm. – (Publication of the American Dialect Society :
   no. 79)
      ISBN 0-8173-0825-3 (pbk.)
      1. English language—Dialects—Research—Law and legisla-
tion—United States.   2. Dialectology—Research—Law and legislation—
United States.   3. English language—Dialects—Research—Moral and
ethical aspects—United States.   4. Dialectology—Research—Moral and
ethical aspects—United States.   I. Murray, Thomas E. (Thomas Edward),
1956—   . II. Ross-Murray, Carmin.   III. Series.
PE1702.A5   no. 79
[KF4280.L35]
427'.973 s—dc20
[344.73'09]
[427'.973 s]
[347.3049]

96-7062

British Library Cataloguing-in-Publication Data available

ACKNOWLEDGMENTS

We wish to thank the Bureau of General Research, Kansas State University, for a small grant that made possible much of the research reported in this monograph; Farrell Library, also at Kansas State University, for allowing us extended access to their LEXIS database terminals and for processing our dozens of interlibrary loan requests quickly and efficiently; Ms. Sarah Bryn Greenwood, a graduate student in the Department of English at Kansas State University, for tracking down a few of our secondary sources; Mr. Joel Charles, who offered us a copy of his "Bibliography of Forensic Titles Pertaining to Sound Recordings" while it was still in manuscript form; Ron Butters, several anonymous reviewers, and especially Allan Metcalf and Don Lance, all of whom provided valuable feedback on earlier drafts of the manuscript; and Len Ashley, Dennis Baron, Ed Callary, Tim Frazer, Kelsie Harder, Don Larmouth, Lise Winer, and the many other colleagues (who wish to remain anonymous) who wrote, called, faxed, or e-mailed us in the months following the publication of *PADS 76*.

I. Introduction

In *Publication of the American Dialect Society 76*, we published an essay entitled "On the Legality and Ethics of Surreptitious Recording" (Murray and Ross-Murray 1992, often cited herein as "*PADS 76*" for convenience). Our goals in that essay were straightforward: first, to provide a primer on federal and state legislation and case law regarding the use of surreptitious recording by linguists, folklorists, and others who wish to gather speech data that are untainted by the subject's awareness of being recorded; second, to advance the philosophical argument that the ethics of such surreptitiousness are situation-bound, and that linguists and other watchers of the language should harbor no compunctions about occasionally using (or, more often, continuing to use) surreptitious methods to gather speech data. Because these latter remarks were, by their very nature, based on personal convictions of right and wrong, we suspect that they will continue to be debated for some time to come. We welcome all such discussion, but in this monograph we will have little more to say about that issue.

We write "little more" because we do feel compelled to address the response offered by Roger Shuy in his review of *PADS 76* (1993). Shuy finds our ethical stance illogical and "confusing." After citing two passages from our essay, the first of which admits that surreptitious recording is immoral and the second of which claims that it is not ethically wrong for linguists to engage in surreptitious recording, Shuy writes, "[a]re we to believe that such recording practices are on the one hand immoral but on the other hand ethical? Is there a typographical deus ex machina to save the day here? Or are we missing some subtle distinction of moral (or legal) philosophy?" (104).

In a paper delivered to the national meeting of the American Dialect Society several months following the publication of that review (Murray 1993), Tom Murray noted that the answer to the first of these questions is, of course, yes, for that is precisely the position that the philosophy of situational ethics affords us (see *PADS 76*, 48–50). Most people would agree, for example, that killing another human being is morally wrong; indeed, the United States and most other countries have legal codes that prescribe severe penalties for such actions. Given the proper context, however—in defense of one's life, for example, or even one's political and ideological beliefs (over which numerous wars have been and continue to be fought)—those same people not only believe the killing of another human being to be ethical, they actually sanction such behavior. In *PADS 76*, we merely made the same point with regard to surreptitious recording: it is inherently wrong, but can be sanctioned under certain circumstances.

The last of Shuy's questions—the one in which he asks whether he has missed "some subtle distinction of moral (or legal) philosophy"—we cannot address except to say that the philosophy of situational ethics is not all that subtle, and neither was our statement of it in *PADS 76*.[1]

For the remainder of this essay we will focus on the legality of surreptitious recording. We completed the research for that portion of our *PADS 76* essay in March of 1988, and submitted the final manuscript to *PADS* for consideration the following month. Unfortunately, editorial delays took an especially heavy toll, and the essay did not appear in print until four years later. And between 1988 and 1992, of course, additional legislation was passed and new judicial decisions rendered—this is to be expected in all areas of the law, but especially those such as surreptitious recording, in which the subject matter is so heavily influenced by new technology—so that some portions of our article were obsolete immediately on publication. Thus the need for this companion essay.

In answer to the inevitable question of whether the present study will also be outdated by the time it is published, we can say only that this is an ongoing problem in reporting "current" legal scholarship, just as it is in reporting "current" research in dialectology and sociolinguistics. The legislation and case law cited in this essay were researched during the summer and fall of 1994; the judicial decisions were shepardized during the end of March and beginning of April 1995 (*shepardized* is legal jargon for 'updated; checked for appeals, overrulings, etc.'; it is an eponymous derivation from *Shepard, Shepard's Citations* being a standard reference work in law).

The essay is necessary for other reasons as well. First, we received more than 60 responses to the "legality" portion of *PADS 76*, nearly all of which were sent by colleagues wondering about the legality of surreptitious recording in situations not akin to any we had discussed (see *PADS 76*, 34–45), posing questions of legal fact that had not occurred to us, or merely asking for additional information on one topic or another. (Most queries immediately followed the publication of *PADS 76*; a few others arrived after Shuy's review was printed in the Spring 1993 issue of *American Speech*; and the remainder were prompted by a call for comments, questions, and suggestions that appeared in the *Newsletter of the American Dialect Society* [26.1 (Jan. 1994): 16].) Second, much to our chagrin and in spite of considerable effort to avoid them, the essay in *PADS 76* contains some errors—none glaring, most typographical—that need correcting. Finally, so many colleagues asked specifically about two topics—the legality of surreptitious recording in Canada and the legality of surreptitious video recording (for the study of kinesics, proxemics, and haptics)—that we feel called upon to discuss them as well.

The organization of the present essay is straightforward. Following this introduction, section II will quickly review the federal legislation and case law presented in *PADS 76*, focusing especially on the crucial years 1968–88. Section III will discuss the federal case law (no new relevant federal legislation has been passed), and section IV the various states' legislation and case law since 1988. Section V will address the various questions posed by colleagues following the publication of *PADS 76*. Section VI will broach the legality of surreptitious recording in Canada, and section VII will take up the legality of surreptitious video recording. Finally, section VIII will speculate on whether surreptitious recording can long remain a viable means of gathering linguistic data.

As with *PADS 76*, of course, all the opinions and interpretations we present here are our own unless we state otherwise, and under no circumstances should be construed as specific legal advice.

II. A Review of the Federal Legislation and Case Law to 1988[2]

Prior to 1968, federal statutes governing eavesdropping were spotty, and the case law inconsistent. The first legislation, written in 1917, protected governmental communications only; it did not deal with "private" conversations or the use of surreptitious listening as an investigative tool (see 40 Stat. 1017 [1918]; 56 Cong. Rec. 10761–65 [1918]). Then in 1928, the Supreme Court ruled that telephonic wiretapping by a law enforcement agency was not a "search and seizure," and so did not violate the Fourth or Fifth Amendments (*Olmstead v. U.S.*). But shortly thereafter, Congress enacted §605 of the Federal Communications Act of 1934 (Pub. L. No. 73-652, 48 Stat. 1103 [1934], now 47 U.S.C.A. 605 [1970]), which made all nonconsensual interceptions and disclosures of telephonic communications illegal; and that statute was later upheld by the Supreme Court (*Nardonne v. U.S.*, 1937; *Nardonne v. U.S.*, 1939).

During the 1940s and 1950s, as eavesdropping technology and the people who used it grew more sophisticated, the Federal Communications Act of 1934 and years of judicial precedents became obsolete. Finally, in 1967 the Supreme Court dramatically altered the constitutional principles governing the surreptitious monitoring of speech with two landmark decisions. In *Berger v. New York*, the Court opined that "few threats to liberty exist which are greater than that posed by the use of eavesdropping equipment..." (at 60); and in *Katz v. U.S.*, the Court ruled that electronic surveillance DOES constitute a search and seizure since the Fourth Amendment was designed to protect "people, not places" (at 350n5). The Court added, however, that such protection is afforded only if two important conditions are met: "[f]irst that a person have exhibited an actual (subjective) expectation of privacy and, second that the expectation be one that society is prepared to recognize as 'reasonable'" (at 361).

In 1968 Congress passed the Omnibus Crime Control and Safe Streets Act, one part of which, Title III (18 U.S.C., §§2510–20; see *PADS 76*, app. A), legalized certain kinds of eavesdropping for the first time. Along with its legislative history (see Senate Report 1097), Title III presented the courts with a comprehensive foundation on which to rely for the settling of disputes involving "interception" of "wire" or "oral" communications through the use of any "electronic, mechanical, or other device." Regarding the kinds of eavesdropping permitted by people "not acting under color of law", §2511(2)(d) is explicit:

> It shall not be unlawful . . . to intercept a wire, oral, or electronic communication where such person is a party to the communication or where one of the parties to the communication has given prior consent to such interception unless such communication is intercepted for the purpose of committing any criminal or tortious act in violation of the Constitution or laws of the United States or of any State or for the purpose of committing any other injurious act.

With the stage thus set, it remained only for the various federal courts both to uphold the constitutionality of Title III and to interpret the breadth of its coverage.

The courts were soon called upon to do just that. Title III has been found to protect wire conversations involving regular or landline telephones (*U.S. v. Hall*) and regular telephones and mobile radio telephones (*U.S. v. Hall*), for example, but not those involving cordless telephones (*State v. Howard*, 1984) or two mobile telephones (*U.S. v. Hall*). It has also been found to protect many kinds of oral conversations, such as those occurring in one's home (*Silverman v. U.S.*), a hotel room (*U.S. v. Burroughs*), a telephone booth (*Katz v. U.S.*), or a private office (*Berger v. New York*). Specifically excluded from protection, however, are conversations in which the speakers are conversing so loudly that they should reasonably expect to be overheard (*U.S. v. Carroll*).

It is worth noting, regarding all these rulings, that the speakers' "subjective expectation of privacy" mentioned above is controlled neither by their intention to converse in private nor by the location of the conversation, but by factors such as the content and purpose of the conversation, how it was conducted, and what precautions the speakers took against being overheard. On the other hand, the conversation's location is important to the judgment of "reasonableness" imposed by society on the speakers' expectation of privacy.

Cases focusing on the definition of *intercept* have received split decisions from the courts. Is unmonitored recording "interception"? In *U.S. v. Leta, U.S. v. Turk,* and *U.S. v. King,* the answer was affirmative; in *U.S. v. Bynum,* however, the answer was negative. Is the surreptitious recording of a conversation by one of its participants "interception"? In *U.S. v. Harpel* and *Greenfield v. Kootenai County,* the courts said no; but in *U.S. v. Shields, U.S. v. Turk, Boddie v. American Broadcasting Co. (1),* and *U.S. v. Truglio,* the courts said yes. And the question of what is or is not an "electronic, mechanical, or other device," though not addressed comprehensively by the federal courts as of early 1988, also promised confusion. Is a tape recorder such a device? It would seem so, but a Virginia court ruled otherwise (*Cogdill v. Commonwealth*), and other states have specifically mentioned tape recorders in the wording of their statutes. Is an extension phone such a device? One would think so, but the federal courts have said no, as long as the extension phone in question is "installed normally" and "receiving normal use" (*U.S. v. Christman* and *Anonymous v. Anonymous*).

As for judicial rulings specifically involving §2511(2)(d) of Title III, the decisions have been numerous and varied. In *Meredith v. Gavin,* for example, the Eighth Circuit held that a one-party consensual recording later admitted as evidence against the party who had been recorded surreptitiously nevertheless did not violate Title III since the original purpose of the recording was not "criminal or tortious." The court also observed in the same ruling that "the preservation of an accurate record for important purposes . . . [is] not [an] injurious act" (at 799). On the other hand, more than one court has ruled that a person's "right to be left alone" is sacred, and that "invasion of privacy" is a tortious act under Title III (see, for example, *Galella v. Onassis, Nader v. General Motors Corp.,* and *Brown v. American Broadcasting Co.*).

In *Smith v. State,* the Supreme Court affirmed that a one-party consensual recording later transcribed and printed in a newspaper did not violate Title III because the defendant, as a "party to the conversation," could easily have repeated it verbatim from memory, and because, in any case, a party to a conversation is guilty neither of "eavesdropping" nor "wiretapping" when he or she records that conversation. And as for the meaning of *party to a conversation,* it has been held that "witnesses" to conversations are "parties" even if they do not speak (*Grandbouche v. Adams*) and that "visibility" to the speakers rather than actual "participation" is the salient factor (*U.S. v. Coven*).

Eavesdropping technology continued to advance, and by the mid-1980s Title III was so far out of date that Congress passed the Electronic Communications Privacy Act of 1986 (ECPA), officially a revision of Title III.[3] The new language (see *PADS 76*, app. B), according to its legislative history (see H. Rep. No. 99-647, 99th Cong., 2nd Sess., 1986), was intended to protect non-wire communications such as those involving computers and cellular telephones; non-voice portions of wire communications such as modem and Telex transfers; most other electronic communications involving the transfer of "intelligence of any nature' not "readily accessible" to or for the use of the general public; and communications on private telephone or electronic communications systems. As of early 1988, most of the new provisions of the ECPA had not yet been tested in the courts.

The ECPA also changed Title III in a way that escaped our attention in the earlier essay (see *PADS 76*, app. C, 72). As originally enacted, §2511(1) provided that a person could be convicted of violating any federal statute governing surreptitious recording only if he or she had acted "willfully"; but because that term caused confusion in the courts (see, for example, *Malouche v. JH Mgmt. Co.*, *Citron v. Citron*, and *U.S. v. Ross*), the ECPA changed *willfully* to *intentionally*. Senator Patrick Leahy, a co-sponsor of the ECPA, explained that "[w]e wanted to underscore that the inadvertent reception of a protected communication is not a crime. In order to do that, we changed the state of mind requirement . . . from 'willful' to 'intentional'" (132 Cong. Rec. S14,449 [daily ed., 1 Oct. 1986]). And Senator Daniel Mathias stated that "this amendment provides that only intentional acts of interception—those meeting the highest standard of specific intent—can be punished criminally" (132 Cong. Rec. S14,034 [daily ed., 27 Sept. 1986]). Linguists who intercept any kind of communication accidentally therefore have nothing to fear (though the use of such conversations as data could be punishable if the acquisition would have been illegal had it not been accidental; see Meyer 1988, 439–40, and Fishman 1991, 60–62).

III. Federal Case Law Since 1988

We completed the research for the essay in *PADS 76* close enough to the enactment of the ECPA (though signed by President Ronald Reagan on 21 Oct. 1986, it did not become law until 20 Jan. 1987) that—as noted earlier—many of its components had not yet been tested in the courts. Eight years later, though ECPA-related case law is still relatively meager, enough judicial precedents have been set that the future behavior of the courts in this area, though not entirely predictable, is indicated. We feel obliged to review these precedents so that linguists who may have reason to record data surreptitiously and who wish to abide by the law will have clearer guidelines to follow. In keeping with the pattern established in *PADS 76*, we will therefore discuss the relevant paragraphs of §§2510 and 2511 of the revised Title III, and the corresponding case law, in chronological order (we usually provide only parenthetical summaries of the statutes at each subheading; for more detailed language, see apps. B and C in *PADS 76*, 69–75, but see also below for some emendations to that language). For those portions of §§2510 or 2511 not appearing below, readers may assume that no significant changes have occurred since 1988. We will, of course, have to make judgments concerning which changes are pertinent to linguists gathering speech data and which are not. Indeed, more than a few of the letters we received from colleagues following the publication of *PADS 76* asked questions regarding the legality of listening and recording activities that we had not envisioned. We will try to think less conservatively in the discussions that follow.

As a general precursor, we once again remind readers that, as Carr (1991–92, 3: 3)[4] says, "[a]ny activity not encompassed in a definition in §2510 is not included within Title III's statutory and regulatory framework. If not covered by Title III, the activity is [not] prohibited ... except as may be necessitated by another statute or the Constitution."

§2510(1) [DEFINITION OF *WIRE COMMUNICATION*]

In *PADS 76,* the definition of *wire communication* as amended by the ECPA was incomplete and thereby misleading (69). We therefore begin this section with a corrected definition:

any aural transfer made in whole or in part through the use of facilities for the transmission of communications by the aid of wire, cable, or other like connection between the point of origin and the point of reception (including the use of such connection in a switching station) furnished or operated by any person engaged in providing or operating such facilities for the transmission of interstate or foreign communications, or communications affecting interstate or foreign commerce; and such term includes any electronic storage of such communication, but such term does not include the radio portion of a cordless telephone communication that is transmitted between the cordless telephone handset and the base unit.

We regret the error, though our discussion in *PADS 76* was based on the correct form of the definition.

In *People v. Fata,* the court established, predictably, that non-wire communications do not include those carried by cordless telephones; in fact, the ruling judge opined that "those who use cordless telephones do so at their peril." Such conversations are therefore not automatically protected by Title III and will be treated as "oral" in nature (and so are subject to the same two-part test involving the speaker's expectation of privacy and society's willingness to accept that expectation as "reasonable"). In general, however, as Strugatz (1990, 1152, 1156–57) states, "users of cordless telephones have no justifiable expectation of privacy for their conversations" because they are aware that their conversations are being transmitted by cordless telephones. That comment follows a ruling by the Eighth Circuit Court of Appeals in *Tyler v. Berodt* that neither the Fourth Amendment (all people are guaranteed freedom from unreasonable search and seizure), the Fourteenth

Amendment (all people are guaranteed equal protection under the law), Title III (even as unamended by the ECPA), nor 42 U.S.C.S. §1983 (providing cause of action for unconstitutional invasion of privacy) protects conversations on cordless telephones from surreptitious interception and recording. Left unsettled is whether conversations carried by one cordless telephone and one wire telephone (that is, conversations in which one party is unaware that the conversation is, in part, wireless) are protected, though the court in *Tyler v. Berodt* (at 706–07n2) opined that they are "generally thought" to be (see also *State v. Howard* [1990], *State v. Delaurier*, and Robinson 1991).

§2510(2) [DEFINITION OF *ORAL COMMUNICATION*]

That words "knowingly exposed to the public, even in [one's] ... own home or office" are not protected by the Fourth Amendment or Title III has been well-established; similarly, statements that a person "exposes to the 'plain view' of outsiders are not 'protected' because no intention to keep them to himself has been exhibited" (*Katz v. U.S.* at 359, 361). But now the Seventh Circuit has affirmed, as Carr (1991–92, 3: 10) says, that "a person who has no reasonable basis for believing that his conversations are not being overheard likewise has no reasonable basis for believing that they are not being recorded" (*In re John Doe Trader No. One*). This is true even if the recording occurs on premises that have an institutional rule prohibiting the use of tape recorders (*In re John Doe Trader No. One*; as Fishman 1991, 183, points out, "[t]he court noted that the rule against tape recorders may have been intended primarily as a noise control measure"). To the list of contexts that are typically assumed to be private and free of intrusion, however (see *PADS 76*, 22), we can add "any area of a business set aside for private activities" (*La Porte v. State*; the particular area in question in this case was a dressing room used by models to change clothes), but not a public jail (*Angel v. Williams*) or a police car (*U.S. v. McKinnon*). Finally, neither the content of a conversation (*La Porte v. State*) nor the language in which the conversation is held (*People v. Siripongs*) has any bearing on whether the conversation is statutorily protected from surreptitious interception. (It is worth noting, however, that in *People v. Siripongs* the person doing the surreptitious recording was a police officer. This may or may not have influenced the court's ruling.)

§2510(4) [DEFINITION OF *INTERCEPT*]

The "interception" of a communication now involves an individual's illegal use of an "electronic, mechanical, or other device" as defined either in §2510(5) *or* the "correlative provision of a state ... statute" (Carr 1991–92, 3: 21; see *Commonwealth v. Brachbill*). In other words, the courts have broadened the definition of *or other device* to include state-defined "devices." It has also been held that a person who records conversations that are overheard without benefit of any amplifying device is NOT guilty of "interception" (*Mimms v. Mimms*), though he or she IS still constrained by the statutory and judicial standards for privacy in "oral" conversations. Finally, Carr (1991–92, 3: 39–40; footnotes omitted, but paraphrased in brackets) makes a pertinent observation that is worth citing at length:

> The phrase *aural acquisition* [italics added] ... could be interpreted to include listening to previously recorded conversations. On its face, §2510(4) is not restricted to the act of initial overhearing or recording at the time the conversation occurred [*U.S. v. Turk*]. Nonetheless, the central concern of Title III is the interceptor's eavesdropping at the time of the conversations. If each replaying of a recording involved a new interception, countless interceptions could arise from a single conversation. Furthermore, to consider the act of replaying an interception is to disregard the statute's distinction between interception and disclosure, apparent in §2511 and §2517. The act of surveillance was the primary congressional concern, and replaying of previously recorded conversations is a disclosure, not an interception, of those communications [*U.S. v. Turk*].

Linguists who may listen to their colleagues' illegally procured data—as, for example, at a conference—therefore have nothing to fear; the same is true for students who may be asked to listen to such data in classrooms, spouses and children who may (intentionally or not) hear it at home, and so forth.

§2510(5) [DEFINITION OF *ELECTRONIC, MECHANICAL, OR OTHER DEVICE*]

In *PADS 76* (69), our definition of *electronic, mechanical, or other device* as amended by the ECPA was not accurately printed. We therefore begin this section with a corrected definition:

> any device or apparatus which can be used to intercept a wire or oral communication other than (a) any telephone or telegraph instrument, equipment or facility, or any component thereof. . . .

Again, we regret the error, though our discussion in *PADS 76* was based on the correct definition.

A significant though controversial judicial precedent has been extended: an extension telephone used without the knowledge or consent of either party to a conversation is not a "device" under this statute (see *PADS 76* [24], *Commonwealth v. Hammond, State v. Reyes*, and especially *Scheib v. Grant*, which was tried in a federal district court and later denied a hearing in the Supreme Court), even under circumstances in which one-party consensual recording otherwise would have been illegal under state law (see *Commonwealth v. Brachbill*, and note Carr's opinion that "[i]f these cases allow an 'extension phone exception' to Title III to develop, the purpose of the statute to regulate secret eavesdropping could be substantially undone" [1991–92, 3-42.2]).

Whether a tape recorder constitutes a "device" under this statute apparently differs from jurisdiction to jurisdiction and context to context. We cite Fishman (1991, 35; footnotes omitted, but summarized in brackets) on the matter:

> Several federal courts have concluded that to tape record a conversation does not constitute an interception of it, so long as the person who recorded the conversation overheard it lawfully [see, most recently, *In Re John Doe Trader Number One*]. . . . [¶] Other federal . . . courts, however, [have held] that such recordings do constitute interceptions, even in consensual interception situations [see, most recently, *Walker v. Darby*]. [¶] The Eleventh Circuit has held that to record a conversation and to transmit it (using separate equipment) can constitute two interceptions [*U.S. v. Shields*].

Of greatest interest to linguists, however, may be the fact that there have been no questions of legal culpability for people who tape record conversations lawfully and then, before they use the conversations (for whatever purpose), obtain the consent of the person(s) recorded. See also Bindler (1992, 858–59), *Royal Health Care Servs., Inc. v. Jefferson-Pilot Life Ins. Co.*, and *Epps v. St. Mary's Hospital, Inc.*

§2510(12) [DEFINITION OF *ELECTRONIC COMMUNICATION*]

The most obvious application of this section of Title III is to communications such as electronic mail (e-mail). (Such communications, though technically conveyed through telephone wires, are considered "non-wire" by §2510[1] because they are not aural.) Though this aspect of §2510 still seems not to have been tested in the federal courts—dozens of cases involving the alleged monitoring, theft, or tampering of an individual's e-mail have been filed, of course, but none of the subsequent rulings has depended specifically on the meaning of *electronic communication*—a complaint was filed in 1988 which, if it had not been subsequently withdrawn, would certainly have required a ruling in the Southern District Court of Indiana (see *Thompson v. Predaina*). Hernandez (1988, 33; footnotes omitted) summarizes the facts of the complaint:

> ... Thompson was exchanging private e-mail via an 'echo' intermail networked conference on Predaina's BBS system. After reading the messages she received, she routinely deleted them. Predaina, however, allegedly restored the private e-mail and caused the e-mail to become public. The e-mail was also allegedly echoed publicly on other BBS's along the network.

Thompson filed three separate federal claims, two of which were under the ECPA (the third was under the Cable Communications Act of 1984, and need not concern us here): one contends that Predaina violated 18 U.S.C. 2520(a) by "intercept[ing], disclos[ing], or intentionally us[ing] in violation of this chapter" Thompson's "electronic communications"; the other contends that Predaina violated 18 U.S.C. 2707(a) by accessing Thompson's STORED "electronic communications" "with a knowing or intentional state of mind" (see Hernandez 1988, 35). The validity of both complaints, of course, ultimately turns on the definition of *electronic communication,* and as Hernandez (1988) makes clear, the court would certainly have found Thompson's e-mail communications to lie within the purview of that phrase.

Another issue involving this statute has received some judicial attention. As Carr (1991–92, 3: 20) points out, "[t]he definition [of *electronic communication*] contains exceptions for the radio portion of a cordless telephone transmission between the handset and a base station, wire or oral communications, tone-only paging device communications, and tracking device communications" (see 2510[12][A], [B], [C], and [D]). The Eighth Circuit Court of Appeals has found that listening to a conversation transmitted by a cordless telephone therefore does not violate the statute (*Tyler v. Berodt*, and see also *People v. Fata* and *State v. Smith*).

§2511(1)(A), (B), (C), (D) [LEGALITY OF INTERCEPTION AND DISCLOSURE OF WIRE, ORAL, OR ELECTRONIC COMMUNICATIONS]

We did not explicitly discuss §2511(1)(a), (b), (c), or (d) in *PADS 76*, though we did include them in Appendix C (72) as specifying federal penalties and/or limitations for the surreptitious interception and disclosure of communication. We have already addressed the fact that the first word of each of the four paragraphs should have been *intentionally* (see the end of section II in the present essay); here we wish to note that some other omissions and oversights also occurred in paragraphs (c) and (d). We therefore offer the following corrected language for all four paragraphs:

(1) Except as otherwise specifically provided in this chapter any person who—
(a) intentionally intercepts, endeavors to intercept, or procures any other person to intercept or endeavor to intercept, any wire or oral communication;
(b) intentionally uses, endeavors to use, or procures any other person to use or endeavor to use any electronic, mechanical, or other device to intercept any oral communication when—. . . ;
[Subparagraphs (i)–(v), which list the specific circumstances under which paragraph (b) is enforceable, are omitted here both because they are irrelevant to our discussion and because they are printed correctly in *PADS 76* (app. C, 72).]
(c) intentionally discloses, or endeavors to disclose, to any other person the contents of any wire, oral, or electronic communication, knowing or having reason to know that the information was obtained through the interception of a wire, oral, or electronic communication in violation of this subsection; or

(d) intentionally uses, or endeavors to use, the contents of any wire, oral, or electronic communication, knowing or having reason to know that the information was obtained through the interception of a wire, oral, or electronic communication in violation of this subsection; shall be punished as provided in subsection (4) or shall be subject to suit as provided in subsection (5).

We regret the errors; however, they did not affect our discussion of the pertinent issues in *PADS 76*.

Paragraphs (a), (b), (c), and (d) are separated from one another by semicolons, and the word OR precedes (d). Common sense therefore dictates that each of the paragraphs delineates a crime separate from the others, and that a person could be punished after being found guilty of any one of them. Interestingly, however, the courts have not always followed this logic in their rulings, and have thus created a problematic set of judicial precedents. Since some linguists may, for example, have participated in illegal surreptitious recording without ever having used or divulged their data, the question of whether (a), (b), (c), and (d) should be interpreted as separate crimes or as somehow linked is worthy of our attention here.

The answer to this question seems to be rooted in the 1982 case of *By-Prod Corp. v. Armen-Berry*, in which the defendant intentionally recorded a conversation illegally but never used the recording (and in fact erased it shortly after recording it). In finding for the defendant, the Seventh Circuit Court of Appeals issued the following dictum (at 960):

We doubt . . . that a tape recording which was never used could form the basis for liability under section 2511(2)(d). It would be a dryly literal reading of the statute that found a violation because at the moment of pressing the "on" button a party to a conversation conceived an evil purpose though two seconds later he pressed the "off" button and promptly erased the two seconds of tape without even playing it back. A statute that provides for minimum damages of $1000 per violation must have more substantial objects in view than punishing evil purposes so divorced from any possibility of actual harm. We think it is the use of the interception with intent to harm rather than the fact of interception that is critical to liability, and there was no use of the interception here.

As Render and McClure (1991, 440) make clear, the court rendered this opinion "without any supporting case law."

In 1984, however, faced with a similar set of circumstances in *Boddie v. American Broadcasting Co.*, the Sixth Circuit Court reached a different conclusion (at 339, emphasis added):

> The Wiretap Statute requires the plaintiff to show that the defendants intended an illegal, tortious or injurious act other than the recording of the conversation. Even if we assume that the defendants, by the mere interception, violated these [F.C.C.] regulations, the question remains under §2511(2)(d) whether the defendants INTENDED TO USE the recorded conversation to injure Boddie.

Thus the Sixth Circuit seemed to opine that ACTUAL use is not a requirement for violation of Title III; INTENDED use suffices to meet the statute's requirement for liability. But in 1989, that opinion changed: in its ruling on a second *Boddie v. American Broadcasting Co.* suit, the Sixth Circuit held (at 270, quoting from *By-Prod. v. Armen-Berry*, no less) that "[w]hile the statute on its face does not punish the use of communications, as a practical matter it is doubtful that a tape-recording which was never used could form the basis for liability under section 2511(2)(d)." Nevertheless, just six months later the same court ruled, in *Stockler v. Garratt* (at 859), that the actual use of a recording is not a requirement for violation of Title III, but that the simple act of interception is sufficient:

> The statute does not by its terms . . . [require] that the recording actually be used. This omission cannot be assigned to a scrivener's error and, of course, if actual use was intended to be required, Congress can readily amend the statute to so provide. While we recognize that, without requiring use of the interception, it will be a problem, as here, to determine the purpose, it can hardly be said that, as written, the statute does not make sense. We hold, therefore, that it is not necessary for liability that the interception be used for a criminal or tortious purpose.

Although this decision has subsequently been cited with approval in yet another Sixth Circuit case (*In re King World Prods., Inc.*, at 59), has found favor with at least two legal scholars (Render and McClure 1991, 452–53), and seems to fulfill the legislative intent underlying the drafting of Title III (Senate Report No. 1097 at 2236, and 114 Cong. Rec. 14694 [1968]), we believe that there has been too much waffling on the issue to draw any firm conclusions. As Chief Judge Merritt wrote in his dissenting opinion in *Stockler v. Garratt* (at 860), the judicial inconsistency thus far will almost certainly require a Supreme Court resolution. (The second *Boddie*

v. *American Broadcasting Co.* case was appealed to the Supreme Court in 1990, but was denied a hearing. Such a denial does not imply tacit approval of the Circuit Court's ruling, however; indeed, in recent years the Supreme Court has agreed to hear fewer than 100 of the approximately 7,000 cases brought before it annually [McAllister 1995, 26]. The Court may simply be waiting for additional judicial pressure to mount, or even for what it believes to be a more opportune socio-political climate to appear, before it tackles the issue. As McAllister notes, "the Supreme Court has complete discretion to deny a . . . petition for any reason, or for no reason at all"; and, in fact, there is a "heavy presumption on the part of the Justices and [their] law clerks that the appropriate disposition of a . . . petition is to *deny* it" [1995, 30 emphasis in original; cf. also 34–35].)

§2511(2)(D) [LEGALITY FOR PEOPLE "NOT ACTING UNDER COLOR OF LAW" TO INTERCEPT WIRE, ORAL, OR ELECTRONIC COMMUNICATIONS]

Several issues require notice here, first among which is whether "prior consent" can ever be implicit (the statute states that a nonparty to a conversation judged to be private must receive the "prior consent" of one of the conversants before undertaking to legally record that conversation). Actually, the issue of implied consent arises most frequently when a police officer seeks the cooperation of an informant, but many of the judicial rulings in such cases are also applicable to linguists and others "not acting under color of law."

The answer is yes: at least one court, for example, has ruled that "implied consent" exists if the interlocutors in a given conversation are aware that they are being recorded and do not object (*U.S. v. Gomez*). As Baumhart (1992, 934) notes, however, citing *Deal v. Spears*, "consent will not be implied solely because a party to the communication 'should have known' that monitoring was a possibility." Moreover, though an employer may give consent for conversations in the workplace that he or she oversees to be monitored, that consent does not automatically extend to all the conversations of all the employees, especially if the manner of monitoring is not fully disclosed (*Williams v. Poulos*).

A linguist wishing to record any conversation in which he or she is not a participant would always be best advised to obtain the formal, explicit (and uncoerced; see *Arnold v. State* and *State v. Dimeo*) consent of at least one of the conversants, preferably in writing, for the doctrine of implied consent is exceedingly complex. Indeed, one court has recently opined that no "all-purpose definition" of implied consent is possible (*Griggs-Ryan v. Smith* at 112). The same court said (at 116, 117) that, generally speaking, implied consent exists "where a person's behavior manifests acquiescence or a comparable voluntary diminution of his or her otherwise protected rights," which behavior would include "language or acts which tend to prove (or disprove) that a party knows of, or assents to encroachments on the routine expectation that conversations are private." In sum, however, the court noted (at 119) that the scope of consent depends on the facts peculiar to each case. See also Fishman (1991, 217–20) and Bindler (1992, 862–66).

The second issue arising here is whether the violation of a state statute prohibiting surreptitious recording of one-party consensual conversations also violates §2511(2)(d) of Title III (assuming a federal nexus; that is, assuming that "the activity under scrutiny has a connection with the federal government sufficient to bring that activity within the ambit of federal law" [*PADS* 76, 61n6]), under which such recording is ordinarily considered legal. The answer is a qualified yes. As Carr (1991–92, 3: 86) explains, the reason is because the recording would then have been undertaken "with a criminal purpose," which of course Title III does not permit (*Hirschey v. Menlow*). We hedge in our answer only because the case law on such situations to date is limited to specifically "oral" conversations (that is, those that are non-wire and non-electronic), and any extrapolation, regardless of how logical it may seem, would be risky.

Another issue is whether a person with mixed motives—some honorable, some tortious or even criminal—who records surreptitiously has broken the law. A simple reading of the statute would suggest so, since it forbids any interception of communication done "for the purpose of committing any criminal or tortious act"; but the answer to the question is not nearly so clearcut. For a violation of Title III to occur, the prosecution must prove "either (1) that the PRIMARY motivation, or (2) a DETERMINATIVE factor in the actor's motivation for intercepting the conversation was to commit a criminal, tortious, or other injurious act" (*Hirsche*y *v. Menlow* at 904; emphasis added). Clearly, however, even in the face of such a judicial precedent, the wisest course of action for linguists would be to record only for the purpose of gathering data.

Finally, an issue has arisen involving the convergence of this section and the First Amendment (which promises, among other things, that "Congress shall make no law . . . abridging the freedom . . . of the press . . ."): Specifically, does the First Amendment allow a reporter to surreptitiously record interviews with a source in a state that prohibits one-party consensual recording? The Ninth Circuit Court of Appeals has ruled in the negative (*U.S. v. Aguilar*); other Circuit Court (and, eventually, Supreme Court) rulings will surely be forthcoming.

§2520 [RECOVERY OF CIVIL DAMAGES AUTHORIZED]

In *PADS 76* (75), we mistakenly noted the amount of damages provided the plaintiff by §2520(c)(A) if the defendant "has not previously been enjoined under section 2511(5) and has not been found liable in a prior civil action" under that section. The statute stipulates that "the court shall assess the greater of the sum of actual damages suffered by the plaintiff, or statutory damages of not less than $50 and not more than $500." We regret the error, though it did not affect our discussion in *PADS 76*.

Two new issues have arisen with regard to §2520. First, if a linguist is convicted of participating in a type of surreptitious recording that has been judged by a court of law to be illegal, of course he or she would be subject to criminal penalties; and if the offended party wished to sue, a court could award civil damages as well. Regarding the latter, as Carr (1991–92, 8: 41) says, "[u]nder §2520 [see *PADS 76*, 74–75], actual damages can be awarded to the successful plaintiff, but such damages shall not be less than liquidated damages computed at the rate of $100 a day for each day of violation or $1,000, whichever is higher." But a question remains: What if "actual damages" have not been established? In that case, according to the Eleventh Circuit (*Dunn v. Blue Ridge Telephone Co.*), the award for damages cannot exceed the number of days interception occurred, at $100 per day, or the number of interceptions, at $1,000 each, whichever is greater. And according to the Seventh Circuit (*Rodgers v. Wood*), damages are mandatory under the statute; a court does not have the discretion to decline an award. Provided these judicial precedents are followed, an unsuccessful defendant would therefore be ordered to pay a fine of at least $100, and perhaps a great deal more.

The second issue under this statute concerns time limits. Paragraph (e) explicitly states that civil actions must be filed within "two years after the date upon which the claimant first has a reasonable opportunity to discover the violation." But if two or more linguists are working on a project together, and the plaintiff "discovers the violation" of only one of them, does the two-year clock begin ticking on all of them or only on the one caught? Carr (1991–92, 8: 25–26; footnotes omitted) provides the answer, summarizing the findings of the Eighth Circuit Court of Appeals in *Andes v. Knox*: "[t]he period of limitations begins to run from the date the plaintiff is aware of the violation, even if at that time he or she is not aware of the identities of all the potential defendants. At that point, suit may be filed and the identities of the other persons who may be liable can be learned through discovery." (By the way, the two-year period of limitations cited in this statute does not apply retroactively to illegal surveillance done before the enactment of the ECPA; see *Scutieri v. Estate of Revitz*.)

At the risk of stating the obvious, we wish to note that any conclusion to this section would be illusory: the accumulation of case law is ongoing; "[t]he Supreme Court can and does occasionally overrule its own decisions" (McAllister 1995, 39); and judicial precedents can be overturned or rendered moot by the passage of new legislation. And certainly Title III will receive continued attention in the courts and in Congress as the various kinds of devices used to surreptitiously intercept communication become increasingly sophisticated.

IV. State Legislation and Case Law Since 1988

As we mentioned in section I, since 1988 many state legislatures and courts have passed new statutes and/or rendered new judicial decisions that bear directly on the use of surreptitious recording as a method of gathering linguistic data, and in this section we will summarize that legislation and case law (we recommend, however, that readers examine the complete language of the statutes governing their state in conjunction with our synopsis). We will also make a few minor typographical corrections to the statute numbers reported in *PADS 76*, and, in response to readers' queries, attempt to provide a bit more detail for some of the states.

One subject that we have consciously avoided in preparing this section (as well as its corollary in *PADS 76*) is the surreptitious monitoring of the language of people who have been arrested, detained, or incarcerated. We recognize that some colleagues have studied the language of such people, but the available statutes and case law address the issue only from the perspective of what is allowable by people "acting under color of law"—that is, people acting as (or under the jurisdiction of) law enforcement officers. Indeed, most states have separate provisions in their statutes for such people (as does Title III; see §2511[2][c]), and we have omitted such provisions from our discussion, both here and in *PADS 76*.

Again, we remind readers that the statutes and judicial decisions cited below prevail only if no federal nexus can be shown to exist. All of our comments in this section pertain to one-party consensual recording, and, though based in part on Carr (1991–92), actually update that research. (Fishman 1991, 119–50, is another excellent source for interested readers, though his discussion centers primarily on the legality of recordings made by law enforcement officials, and is, in any case, also a bit out of date.) If a state does not appear in the following list, readers may assume that no changes have occurred in its statutes or case law since early 1988. Finally, we must note that this section complements pages 30–34 of the *PADS* essay. To avoid repeating ourselves excessively, we will have to refer to that essay frequently, and readers may wish to do the same.

ALABAMA. As reported in *PADS 76* (30); however, note that the statute prohibiting the use of a device to eavesdrop illegally was found not to be violated by people who listen to transmissions over a specially assigned radio frequency (*Blackmon v. State*).

ALASKA. As reported in *PADS 76* (30); however, see Alaska Stat., §42.20.310, not §42.20.3.10. Note also that Alaska specifically enumerates its citizens' rights to privacy in its constitution, art. I, §22.

ARIZONA. As reported in *PADS 76* (30); however, see Ariz. Rev. Stat. Ann., §§13-3005(1), (2), not §§13.3005(1), (2), and note that the state has no definition of *wire communication* or *oral communication* in its statutes. (Here and elsewhere, if a statute does not specifically define a particular term, the courts will be left to interpret its meaning.) Note also that the statutes expressly forbid "interception" using a tape recorder, and that Arizona specifically enumerates its citizens' rights to privacy in its constitution, art. II, §8.

CALIFORNIA. Still generally prohibited by statute—eavesdropping with "any electronic amplifying or recording device" is illegal (although, interestingly, the statute does not apply to law enforcement personnel, who are permitted to make non-warrant consensual interceptions [see Cal. Penal Code, §§629.38, 633])—and upheld in the courts (in *Ribas v. Clark*, for example, in which it was held that the use of an extension phone to eavesdrop, even with the consent of one of the parties to the conversation, is unlawful); and a new addition to the statute now specifically prohibits the "malicious interception" of communications involving cellular telephones as well (Cal. Penal Code, §632.5 [Supp.]). One court, however, has recently read §632 of the Penal Code as allowing the one-party consensual recording of a telephone conversation (*Reed v. Dick*), though another court has followed earlier precedents and held that such recording contravenes the statute (*Frio v. Superior Court*). In any event, conversations occurring in contexts in which the speakers do not have a reasonable expectation of privacy are "public" and can be recorded by one of the parties (*U.S. v. Regan*); and conversations in which the parties have no expectation that the discussion would not be disclosed to others are not "confidential" (*People v. Pedersen*). Finally, the consent of the telephone company is required before even two-party consensual tapping can be done (*People v. Jones*). See also Pennypacker (1989), *People v. Otto*, and *Bunnell v. Superior Court*, and note that California specifically enumerates its citizens' rights to privacy in its constitution, art. I, §1.

CONNECTICUT. Though the legislation reported in *PADS 76* was subsequently upheld by the state's supreme court (*State v. Grullon*; see also Atkinson 1991), new legislation now prohibits one-party consensual recording; see Conn. Gen. Stat. Ann., §52-570(d)(a)(1), which has been upheld in *State v. McVeigh*.

FLORIDA. As reported in *PADS 76* (31), but note that the state has a definition of *oral communication* that specifically exempts "any public oral communication uttered at a public meeting." Note also that Florida specifically enumerates its citizens' rights to privacy in its constitution, art. I, §§12, 23.

GEORGIA. As reported in *PADS 76* (31), but note that the state has no definition of *wire communication* or *oral communication* in its statutes. Note also that the statutes expressly forbid "interception" using a tape recorder, and that tape recorders are included in the definition of *electronic, mechanical, or other device*.

HAWAII. Still permitted by statute, though a specific definition of *wireless communications*, encompassing cellular telephones, has been adopted; see Haw. Rev. Stat. Ann. §803-41 (Supp.). Note also that Hawaii specifically enumerates its citizens' rights to privacy in its constitution, art. I, §§6–7.

IDAHO. As reported in *PADS 76* (31); in addition to Idaho Code, §18-6703(2)(d)(e), however, see also the related §18-6702(2)(d)(e).

ILLINOIS. Substantially as reported in *PADS 76* (31), but see also Reed (1988), Loeb (1993), *People v. Wilson*, *Bender v. Board of Fire & Police Commissioners*, *People v. Wehde*, *People v. Regains*, *People v. White*, and *People v. Schnurr*, and note that the statute has been interpreted as prohibiting eavesdropping only where the conversations or statements were intended to be private (see *People v. Klingenberg*). Note also that although removal of the mouthpiece has been held to convert a telephone into an eavesdropping device (*People v. Gervasi*), such a device is NOT created if the listener simply places a hand over the mouthpiece (*People v. Shinkle*). Moreover, it has been held that a conventional radio scanner capable of receiving an FM signal, including the signal transmitted by a mobile telephone, does not constitute an eavesdropping device (*People v. Wilson*). And contrary to judicial precedent (and to what we reported in *PADS 76*), a court has held that a specific request not to record can be disregarded if the tape recorder is visible to the person who made the request (*Smith v. Associated Bureaus, Inc.*). It may also be worth mentioning that the Illinois legislature has modified its definition of *private oral communication* to protect the privacy of both cordless telephonic and cellular conversations (Ill. Rev. Stat. ch. 38, ¶ 108B-[1][o] [1991]), though the amendment appears in the section of the code dealing with police wiretaps and may therefore apply only to people "acting under color of law." Finally, note that Illinois specifically enumerates its citizens' rights to privacy in its constitution, art. I, §6.

INDIANA. As reported in *PADS 76* (31), but note that the state's definition of *interception* includes tape recording.

IOWA. Still permitted by statute; in addition to Iowa Code Ann., §727.8, however, see also the related §808 B.2(2)(c).

KANSAS. Still technically permitted by statute in contexts in which the person being recorded does not have a reasonable expectation to privacy (see Kan. Stat. Ann., §21-4001), though at least one legal scholar has concluded that Kansas is now effectively a two-party state (see Bindler 1992, 865n88, and *State v. Gibson*).

LOUISIANA. Still permitted by statute, and now upheld in the courts (*State v. West, State v. Tucker*); however, another statute requires the consent of all parties to "eavesdrop or record" confidential communications (see La. Rev. Stat. Ann., §14:322.1[A]; this prohibition does not apply to law enforcement personnel [see La. Rev. Stat. Ann., §14:322.1 D], though the resulting lack of equality has been held to contravene the state's constitution [*Kirk v. State*]). Note also that Louisiana specifically enumerates its citizens' rights to privacy in its constitution, art. I, §5.

MAINE. As reported in *PADS 76* (31); however, the new statute appears as Me. Rev. Stat. Ann., title 15, §§709(A)(B) (Supp.).

MARYLAND. As reported in *PADS 76* (31), but see also Messana (1989) and *Standiford v. Standiford*, and note that the state has no definition of *oral communication* in its statutes.

MASSACHUSETTS. As reported in *PADS 76* (31), but see also *Commonwealth v. Shaeffer* and *Commonwealth v. Penta*, and note that the state has no definition of *oral communication* in its statutes. Note also that its definition of *interception* includes tape recording, and that tape recorders are included in its definition of *electronic, mechanical, or other device*.

MICHIGAN. Still prohibited by statute, as reported in *PADS 76* (32), though the courts continue to allow it (see, e.g., *People v. Collins*). For discussions of the resulting legal confusion, see Carter (1991) and Wade (1992).

MINNESOTA. As reported in *PADS 76* (32), but note that the statute allows the interception by a private party of the radio portion of a cordless telephone communication only if that interception occurs inadvertently.

MISSOURI. In *PADS 76*, we presented conflicting information for Missouri. On page 32, in synopsizing the states' legislation and case law, we said that the state permitted one-party consensual recording only by judicial consent; but on page 34, in the first of our hypothetical scenarios, we said that one-party consensual recording was permitted "both by statute and by judicial consent." In the latter instance we were in error. The statute that Missouri has now enacted—apparently the first of its kind in the state's history—follows the case law cited in *PADS 76* (33) in permitting one-party consensual recording (see Mo. Rev. Stat., §542.400[2][3] [Supp.]).

MONTANA. As reported in *PADS 76* (32), but note also that Montana specifically enumerates its citizens' rights to privacy in its constitution, art. II, §10.

NEBRASKA. As reported in *PADS 76* (32), but see Licata (1988–89) for a discussion of why the statute may soon have to be repealed.

NEVADA. As reported in *PADS 76* (32), but note that one court has now opined that listening in on a telephone extension does not constitute an "interception" (*State v. Reyes*).

NEW JERSEY. As reported in *PADS 76* (32), but see Richman (1987, 178–79, 193–95) for a discussion of how inconsistent enforcement of the statute has led to unequal rights for various of New Jersey's citizens.

NEW MEXICO. As reported in *PADS 76* (32), but note that the state has no definition of *wire communication* in its statutes. Also note that the statutes expressly forbid "interception" using a tape recorder.

NEW YORK. Still permitted by statute, and now upheld in the courts (*Harry R. v. Esther R.*); see also Marcus (1988) and Cohen (1989). Note also that, according to N.Y. Penal Law (see §§250.00 and 250.05.), the recording of a cordless telephone conversation that can be overheard by means of an ordinary radio receiver is illegal; and that the state has no definition of *wire communication* or *oral communication* in its statutes, but that its definition of *interception* includes tape recording.

NORTH CAROLINA. As reported in *PADS 76* (32), but see also *State v. Shaw*, in which the courts allowed a husband to listen to conversations between his wife and children without their consent.

OHIO. Still permitted by statute (but see Ohio Rev. Code Ann., §§2933.53[B][4] and [F][3], not §2933.58 [A], [B]), and now upheld in the courts (*State v. Howard*); see also Bowling (1987), and note that the state has no definition of *oral communication* in its statutes.

OREGON. As reported in *PADS 76* (32); however, the statute has now withstood a challenge of "vagueness" (*State v. Knobel*). Moreover, the courts have decided that although a private party can use a police scanner to listen to departmental transmissions, those transmissions cannot be recorded without the speakers' consent (*State v. Bichsel*). And note that the state's definition of *interception* includes tape recording. See also *State v. Stockfleth*.

PENNSYLVANIA. As reported in *PADS 76* (33), though with the judicial clarifications that no violation of the statutes occurs where a caller knowingly speaks to a recording machine (*Commonwealth v. Rozanski*), an answering machine (*Commonwealth v. De Marco*), or, in the case of a face-to-face conversation, has no reasonable expectation of privacy (*Commonwealth v. Henlen*). See also *Commonwealth v. Schaeffer*.

SOUTH CAROLINA. As reported in *PADS 76* (33), but note also that South Carolina specifically enumerates its citizens' rights to privacy in its constitution, art. I, §10.

TEXAS. As reported in *PADS 76* (33), though with the judicial clarifications that such recordings are admissible in domestic relations cases (*Kotrla v. Kotrla*) as well as criminal cases (*Ward v. State*).

UTAH. As reported in *PADS 76* (33); however, see Utah Code Ann., §77-23A-4(7)(a), (b), and (8) rather than §77-23a-4(2)(c).

VERMONT. Still permitted by lack of prohibitory statute, as reported in *PADS 76* (33), and now by judicial consent as well (*State v. Brooks*).

VIRGINIA. As reported in *PADS 76* (33), but note that a tape recorder attached to a telephone is not an "intercepting device" (*Cogdill v. Commonwealth*; Carr 1991–92, 3: 41 notes that "[i]f such an arrangement were able to record without the presence of a human monitor, its use would conflict with 'interception' as that term's meaning in §2410[4] is properly understood"). On the other hand, a telephone console used to overhear calls between two extension lines *is* such a "device" under the statute (*Epps v. St. Mary's Hospital, Inc.*).

WASHINGTON. As reported in *PADS 76* (33), but see Wash. Rev. Code Ann., §9.73.030(1)(a), (b), and (2)(b) (Supp.) and *State v. Gonzalez*, and note that such recording has been judged to be legal if the conversation being recorded is not "private" (*State v. Slemmer*; cf. also the remarks of the court in *Fordyce v. City of Seattle* [at 792–93]: ". . . it is highly probable that the state courts would interpret R.C.W. 9.73.030 so as not to make criminal the recording of a conversation held in a public street, in voices audible to passersby, by the use of a readily apparent recording device"). Note also that the state has no definition of *wire communication* in its statutes, and that the statutes expressly forbid "interception" using a tape recorder. Finally, Washington specifically enumerates its citizens' rights to privacy in its constitution, art. I, §7.

WEST VIRGINIA. Now permitted by statute and confirmed by case law (see W. Va. Code, §62-1D-3[c][2] [Supp.] and *State v. Dillon*).

WISCONSIN. As reported in *PADS 76* (33), though a court has now held that cordless telephone transmissions *are included* within the definition of *wire communications*, and so are protected from nonconsensual interception (*State v. Smith*; see also *State v. Hamblin*).

WYOMING. As reported in *PADS 76* (33), but now confirmed by case law (*Wyoming Dept. of Employment, Div. of Unemployment Ins. v. Patrick*).

We shall conclude this section simply by echoing an important point that we made in *PADS 76* (33–34). In the complex checks-and-balances world of legislation and judicial decisions, there are precious few absolutes. Just because a state has passed a statute legalizing one-party consensual recording, there is no guarantee that the courts of that state will necessarily find the activity to be constitutional; and, conversely, state judiciaries sometimes uphold behavior that their legislatures have sought to outlaw. Even a history of consistent decisions in the courts of a given state does not necessarily ensure the predictability of future judgments; courts do sometimes overrule their own precedents, and the process of appealing decisions, which may go on for many years, provides the constant possibility that a higher court will turn aside years of judicial history. What all of this means is that although the relevant statutes and case law on surreptitious recording would of course be taken into account by any court before rendering a judgment on a new, related case, that case will ultimately be decided primarily on the basis of the facts peculiar to it.

V. Questions from Colleagues

As we mentioned in our introduction, more than 60 colleagues responded to our essay in *PADS 76*, most with questions concerning facts that we had not discussed, but a few posing additional hypothetical situations in which surreptitious recording might conceivably be used. Two questions—involving the legality of surreptitious recording in Canada and the legality of surreptitious video recording—occurred frequently enough and require long enough answers that we have accorded them their own sections below; the most frequently occurring of the others, however, will be answered more briefly here. We again wish to make it clear that none of these answers constitutes specific legal advice, and that all merely represent our opinions as well as the opinions of those whom we cite.

QUESTION. The state in which I live currently has no legislation covering surreptitious recording. Assuming that one day the congress DOES pass such statutes, will it be possible for them to be less restrictive than Title III?

ANSWER. No. Carr (1991–92, 2: 15) explains that according to the legislative history of Title III (see Senate Report Number 1097 at 2181, 2187, and 2189; and 114 Cong. Rec. 11206), "Congress intended to permit state ... laws to be more restrictive than the federal provisions.... State ... statutes cannot, however, be less restrictive than Title III, nor can they expand the opportunities to conduct surveillance beyond those provided by Title III." See also *Commonwealth v. Vitello, U.S. v. Smith,* and *U.S. v. Mora.*

QUESTION. If, as a citizen of the United States, I travel to another country, am I still governed by the surreptitious recording statutes of the United States? Does the Foreign Intelligence Surveillance Act apply in such a situation?

ANSWER. No to both questions. First, citizens of the United States are generally governed by the laws of whatever country they happen to be in (certain agents of the government do occasionally receive diplomatic immunity, but that is a highly specialized situation not likely to affect most linguists). Regarding Title III, part of its legislative history explicitly states that it is not intended to "regulate activities conducted outside the territorial United States" (see H. Rep. No. 99-647), and the courts have concurred (*U.S. v. Mitro, U.S. v. Peterson, Stowe v. Devoy, U.S. v. Tirinkian, State v. Ford,* and *People v. Nicoletti*). Second, the Foreign Intelligence Surveillance Act of 1978 (see Pub. L. No. 95-511, 92 Stat. 1783 codified at 50 U.S.C., §§1801–11 [1982 and Supp. III 1985], and 18 U.S.C., §§2511, 2518–19 [1982 and Supp. IV 1986]), which is intended to provide the exclusive means of authorizing various kinds of electronic surveillance in other countries, can be invoked only through a complex series of judicial processes and is to be used only by agents of the federal government for purposes of national security. See Cinquegrana (1989) and the many citations therein.

QUESTION. According to §2511(2)(g)(i) of the ECPA (see *PADS* 76, 71), "It shall not be unlawful . . . for any person to intercept or access an electronic communication made through an electronic communication system that is configured so that such electronic communication is readily accessible to the general public." Is *electronic communications system* defined anywhere?

ANSWER. Yes. Section 2510(14) defines *electronic communications system* as "any wire, radio, electromagnetic, photooptical or photoelectronic facilities for the transmission of electronic communications, and any computer facilities or related electronic equipment for the electronic storage of such communications." As Carr (1991–92, 3: 46) points out, this definition corresponds directly to the definition of *electronic communications* given in §2510(12) (see *PADS* 76, 70).

QUESTION. Are all phases of electronic mail (e-mail) communications protected by the ECPA, including stored messages?

ANSWER. Probably so, assuming a federal nexus (otherwise state laws will prevail). The ECPA (see §2701[a][1], [2]) states clearly that it is a criminal offense either to "intentionally [access] without authorization a facility through which an electronic communication service is provided; or intentionally [exceed] an authorization to access that facility; and thereby [obtain] . . . a wire or electronic communication while it is in electronic storage . . ."; and according to §2511(1)(a), it is unlawful to "intentionally [intercept], [endeavor] to intercept, or [procure] any other person to intercept or endeavor to intercept, any wire, oral, or electronic communication. . . ." Thus "stored" e-mail seems to be protected both from interception AND from attempted interception (for the Congressional definition of *electronic storage*, see §2510[17][A], [B]). Indeed, according to the legislative history of the ECPA (see Senate Report Number 541), the statutes also similarly protect all video teleconferences, digitized transmissions, and electronic bulletin boards (but see the following question and answer). We hedge in our answer to this question only because the ECPA has not been held by the courts to protect private parties IN THE WORKPLACE, which is where many linguists might attempt to gather data via e-mail. Indeed, Heredia (1992, 308–09) concludes that

> [c]urrently, no federal statutes exist that directly address workplace electronic monitoring. Attempts to state a cause of action under more favorable state statutes have, at least in one case, failed. Recently, federal courts have barred state invasion of privacy claims brought by employees, stating that privacy in the workplace is a matter left to collective bargaining. A claim under federal privacy rights presents a private employee with a major obstacle; absent state action, a private employee cannot assert constitutional rights.

See also Burnside (1987), Weingarten (1988), Wilkes (1991), Witt (1992), and pages 13–14 in this monograph.

QUESTION. Are electronic bulletin boards protected by the ECPA?

ANSWER. Possibly, but probably not. The legislative history of the ECPA makes it clear that Congress intended for electronic bulletin boards to be exempt from the statute's coverage (see Senate Report No. 99-541 at 36, 1986 US Code, Cong. and Admin. News 3580):

> ... the availability of information about the service, and the readily accessible nature of the service are widely known and the service does not require any special access code or warning to indicate that the information is private. To access a communication in such a public system is not a violation of the Act, since the general public has been "authorized" to do so by the facility provider.

The actual language of the ECPA, however, states that the level of protection accorded electronic bulletin boards varies according to their "accessibility to the general public" (§2511[2][g][i]). Although the precise meaning of that phrase has yet to be decided by the courts, some factors that should affect an electronic bulletin board's "public" or "private" nature include whether its messages are encrypted or scrambled (see §2510[16][A]), whether its messages are transmitted using modulation techniques with essential parameters (so that the operator can protect the integrity of the data; see §2510[16][B]), whether its subscribers use passwords, and whether the system prompts its users to indicate if messages are to be kept private. See Clukey (1988), Hernandez (1988), Fishman (1991, 84), and Witt (1992).

This is a question that will almost certainly receive direct attention from the courts in the near future. As of March 1991, 32,000 public dial-up bulletin-board systems existed in the United States (the first appeared in February 1978 [Warren, Thorwaldson, and Koball 1991, 159]); a little more than three years later, in August 1994, there were 57,000 (Gluck 1994, 24); and by March 1995, the number had grown to nearly 65,000 (this according to the Department of Computing and Network Services at Kansas State University). Two corollary statistics of interest may be, first, that as of July 1994, Internet, the world's largest global computer network, reached nearly 25,000,000 computer users, and was doubling in size annually [Elmer-Dewitt 1994, 50]; and second, that as of August 1994, approximately 35% of all American homes possessed one or more personal computers (Gluck 1994, 24; by spring 1995, it was estimated that 32% of all *Americans* possessed one or more personal computers [Jackson 1995, 80]).

QUESTION. According to *PADS 76* (27), the ECPA protects conversations held on cellular telephones, but not on cordless telephones. Is that really correct?

ANSWER. Yes. According to the legislative history of the ECPA (see Senate Report 1097 at 12, 1986 U.S. Code Cong. and Admin. News at 3566), the rationale for excluding cordless telephones is that "[b]ecause communications made on . . . [them] can be intercepted easily with readily available technologies, such as an AM radio, it would be inappropriate to make the interception of such a communication a criminal offense" (see also Carr 1987, 110). As Meyer (1988, 437; footnotes omitted) and other legal scholars have pointed out, however,

[s]imultaneous protection of cellular mobile telephones and exclusion of cordless telephones is unjustifiable under this rationale; like cordless telephones, cellular mobile telephones transmit unencrypted signals which may be intercepted easily with readily available technologies. Given the similarities between cellular mobile and cordless telephones, logic dictates that the two systems be treated similarly. The ECPA's irrational distinction between the two systems is symptomatic of the contradictions inherent in any attempt to protect the privacy of publicly accessible communications.

Curiously, Congress was well aware of the similarities between the two kinds of telephones when it drafted the ECPA.

QUESTION. Donald W. Larmouth (1992, 7) makes the point, quoting Bethany Dumas, that "[t]he law does not recognize a linguist/informant privilege," then goes on to say that because "there is no way that a fieldworker can protect tape recordings or notes from legal seizure unless he or she is willing to go to prison for contempt of court," there can be no "full guarantee of confidentiality of records." Do you agree?

ANSWER. Yes and no. Dumas and Larmouth are correct in their observation that exchanges between linguists and their informants are not privileged; indeed, to date the courts have held more or less sacred only four kinds of conversations—those between physician and patient, attorney and client, priest and penitent, and spouse and spouse (we say "more or less" because certain conditions must be met for the doctrine of privilege to be invoked, and, as always, exceptions to the general rules are numerous; see Goldsmith and Balmforth 1991). On the other hand, we wish to point out that "legal seizure" cannot occur if the things being subpoenaed do not exist. Linguists typically save all their tapes, notes, and other documents, and perhaps with good reason; but of course all such records COULD be erased or destroyed when the linguist is finished with them. In fact, Fishman (1991, 228) makes the specific point, citing *By-Prod. Corp. v. Armen-Berry Co.* and *Baker v. Cestari* that "it is neither a crime nor civilly actionable for a private person to record a conversation for a lawful purpose and then erase the conversation—even if the tape was erased to enable him to commit perjury." (WE ARE NOT ADVOCATING THE DESTRUCTION OF THESE MATERIALS ONCE THEY HAVE BEEN SUBPOENAED; THAT IS A PUNISHABLE OFFENSE.) There can be no doubt that much good data would be lost forever, but such actions WOULD guarantee the confidentiality of the informants from the courts.

Moreover, Dumas and Larmouth are apparently assuming that the notes and tape recordings in question were made legally, which may not be the case. Let us suppose that a linguist who was unaware of the laws recorded data ILLEGALLY, then was called to testify regarding the contents of those recordings. In this situation, the defendant's attorney would have grounds for suppressing both the tapes and the linguist's testimony (see §§2510[11], 2515, 2517, and 2518[10][a], the last of which reads, in part, "Any aggrieved person in any trial, hearing, or proceeding . . . may move to suppress the contents of any wire or oral communication intercepted . . . or evidence derived therefrom on the grounds that . . . the communication was unlawfully intercepted. . ."; see also *Alderman v. U.S., Cubic Corp. v. Cheney, Nardonne v. U.S., U.S. v. Donovan, U.S. v. Dorfman, U.S. v. Giordano, U.S. v. Horton,* Hendrick 1988, Knowlton 1988, Sapp 1989, Smith 1989, Fishman 1991 [220–23], and Carr 1991–92 [3: 38]). Kopecky (1993, 463–64) also makes the important point that "[a]ccording to *Cubic Corp. v. Cheney,* Congress did not intend for the term 'evidence,' as used in the statute, to be strictly interpreted: even if information from an illicit wiretap is not formally received in evidence, it is subject to a motion to suppress if put before the court."

It is also generally true that "courts are forgiving in situations where no motion to suppress was filed": in *Cubic Corp. v. Cheney,* for example, "illegally obtained evidence was excluded even though the party objecting to the evidence did not file a motion to suppress" (Kopecky 1993, 464). Readers should be aware, however, that even if a recording is made in violation of a state law more restrictive than Title III, it is still admissible in a federal civil trial (*Tarnoff v. Wellington Financial Corp., Montone v. Radio Shack, Div. of Tandy Corp.*). In addition, as Kopecky (1993, 455, 456, 457) notes, "evidence obtained in contravention of §2511 may be admitted for the limited purpose of identification" (*Chappell v. Redding*) "when it [is] instrumental in inducing a coerced settlement" (that is, to prevent extortion and blackmail; see *In re Marriage of Lopp* and *Lopp v. Lopp*) and "for the limited purpose of impeachment" (that is, to prevent witnesses from lying when under oath; see *Walder v. U.S., U.S. v. Havens,* and *Jacks v. State*).

Finally, we are forced to wonder how often a linguist might be in a situation where his or her (legally) taped recordings and other records are actually subpoenaed. Such recordings would first have to contain incriminating information (either civil or criminal); then those recordings would have to come to the attention of an interested third party, such as a prosecutor; and THEN the prosecutor would have to decide that the recordings were important enough to be subpoenaed. All in all, this seems a most unlikely chain of events. (We have not included in this scenario the possibility that the person(s) being recorded would have both the desire and the grounds to sue the linguist directly; but if that were the case, the identity of the informant(s) would no longer be an issue anyway.)

QUESTION. Can Person A authorize Person B to record conversations over which Person A, though not a participant, nevertheless has some control or custody?

ANSWER. Generally, no. One-party consensual recording refers to the consent of one or more "parties to the communication" (§2522[2][c], [d]. For example, the person having custody over a particular telephone cannot legally authorize anyone else to tap it (*Anthony v. U.S.* and *U.S. v. San Martin*, but cf. also *Williams v. Poulos*, in which a CEO's approval sufficed as "consent" for the conversations of his employees to be monitored). On the other hand, the courts have recognized "implied consent" to surreptitious recording in certain situations, such as when a person has been informed that a particular telephone is tapped, later forgets about the tap and uses the telephone, then still later attempts to suppress that which has been recorded (*Griggs-Ryan v. Smith*). We discussed the issue of implied consent further in section III.

QUESTION. According to federal law, can conference calls legally be recorded surreptitiously?

ANSWER. Yes. A federal court has held that for the purposes of Title III, a conference call is the legal equivalent of an extension phone even if all the participants in the call are not aware of one another (*U.S. v. Miller*). And as Fishman (1991, 50) says, "[i]mplicit in this holding is that conference call equipment does not constitute a device [see §2510(4), (5)], at least as used in this case."

QUESTION. If I lend my recording equipment to another linguist who then proceeds to use it illegally, can I be held culpable?

ANSWER. Maybe. Title III, §2512, governs the "manufacture, distribution, possession, or advertising" of any device "the design [of which] renders it primarily useful for the purpose of the surreptitious interception of wire or oral communications." Although there has been some uncertainty over the phrase *primarily useful* (see Senate Report 1097, 1968 U.S. Code and Admin. News 2183-84; *U.S. v. Bast* and *U.S. v. Schweihs*; and Fishman 1991, 52–54), §2512 would probably invoke owner-culpability of the recording equipment if the owner sent it through the mail or in any way transported it across state lines; if the owner knew or "had reason to know" (that is, the circumstances were such that any reasonable person could easily have deduced) that it was going to be used for illegal surreptitious recording (*White v. Weiss*); or if the owner advertised it in any way (such as through a newsletter). Alternatively, if one linguist hands a piece of recording equipment to a colleague in the hallway of their office building, and if the lender is completely unaware of his or her colleague's illegal intentions, then the owner would not be culpable. (Note also that §2512[1] provides that the person found guilty of violating this statute "shall be fined not more than $10,000 or imprisoned not more than five years, or both.")

QUESTION. If a linguist illegally recorded data prior to the ECPA, but is not caught until, say, 1993, would he or she still be tried by the pre-ECPA statutes?

ANSWER. Yes. The effective date of the ECPA was 20 January 1987; it therefore applies to conduct occurring only on or following that date. As Fishman (1991, 55) says, "courts and litigants are still obliged to apply pre-ECPA law with regard to criminal prosecutions and civil actions based on conduct occurring before [that date]" (see also *Scutieri v. Estate of Revitz* and *Tyler v. Berodt*). Since the statute of limitations for criminal offenses involving surreptitious recording is five years (see *PADS 76*, 47), however, there should be no new criminal trials involving the original Title III.

QUESTION. Is it safe to assume that speakers in conversations able to be overheard with the naked ear have forfeited their right to an "expectation of privacy"?

ANSWER. Probably. We concluded our discussion of "oral communications" and speakers' "expectations of privacy" in *PADS 76* (22) by claiming that

> ... most conversations occurring in one's own home (see *Silverman v. U.S.*), a hotel room (see *U.S. v. Burroughs*), a telephone booth (see *Katz v. U.S.*), or a private office (see *Berger v. New York*) are assumed to be private, and their speakers have justifiable expectations of privacy. Specifically excluded, however, are conversations in which the speakers are conversing so loudly that they should reasonably expect to be overheard (see *U.S. v. Carroll*).

We might have explained in more detail the kinds of exclusions referred to in that final sentence. In *U.S. v. Jackson*, for example, testimony was allowed from government agents who had overheard conversations by lying on their motel room floor and pressing their ears to the crack at the bottom of the door connecting their room to the next. The court held that the defendants had forfeited their justifiable expectation of privacy simply because their conversations "were audible to the unaided ears of the ... agents lawfully occupying an adjoining room" (at 1051; the court went on to opine [at 1053] that while the behavior of the agents was not "genteel, ... neither was [it] unconstitutional. Not every breach of etiquette poses a constitutional issue"). The facts were similar in *U.S. v. Fisch*: again the authorities could eavesdrop on conversations in a neighboring motel room only with great effort, and again the court allowed the testimony to stand, ruling (at 1077) that

> [a]ppellants would have us divide the listening room into privileged or burdened areas, and the conversations into degrees of audibility to, we presume, the normal ear, thus a remark heard on the bed arguably admissible, but not those heard at the door, a loud remark admissible, arguably one uttered in "normal" tones, but definitely not one whispered. We find no precedent for a categorization involving such hairsplitting and we are not disposed to create one.

And in *Cox v. State*, the court allowed testimony from police officers who had been able to eavesdrop on conversations occurring inside the defendants' apartment only by pressing their ears against the apartment door. The judgments in these cases (and numerous others) may, as Fishman (1991, 231) supposes, "arouse [our] instinctive indignation," but they are generally supported by legal scholars and, in any case, are the law as it has been interpreted thus far (though the 4th Circuit Court ruled in *Benford v. American Broadcasting Co.* that the issue of privacy expectations is supposed to be resolved on a case-by-case basis). It is also worth noting that all such cases to date have involved law enforcement officials, a fact that may have influenced the various courts' decisions. See also Carr (1991–92, 3: 10–13).

QUESTION. The language of §2511(2)(d) says that certain kinds of surreptitious recording are legal "unless such communication is intercepted for the purpose of committing any criminal or tortious act in violation of the Constitution or laws of the United States or of any State." Can I assume that the District of Columbia is included in the meaning of *State*?

ANSWER. Yes. According to §2510(3), "'State' means any State of the United States, the District of Columbia, the Commonwealth of Puerto Rico, and any territory or possession of the United States."

QUESTION. Can I legally record discourse by placing a tape recorder in a public place (where I can easily overhear conversations with my naked ear), turning it on, leaving it untended, and then returning to it an hour later?

ANSWER. No. Fishman (1991, 231–32) explains that an unmonitored tape recorder does not record what a listener using it has heard, but "aurally acquires" the conversation—that is, it becomes a "device" and is "intercepting" the conversation according to §2510(4), (5). Indeed, the court in *People v. Castania* (at 835) proclaimed that "the human and the electronic ear must co-exist and co-function. When the human ear is turned away, the electronic ear must be turned off." One court has allowed unmonitored interception (*U.S. v. Bynum*), but that ruling is clearly the exception to an otherwise uniform judicial trend. Carr (1991–92, 3: 24) concludes that "[u]nmonitored recording is difficult to describe as anything but an unreasonable seizure of conversations, and therefore unconstitutional under the Fourth Amendment...." See also *U.S. v. Duncan* and *U.S. v. McIntyre*.

QUESTION. In your *PADS 76* essay (44), one of the hypothetical examples centers on "[a] linguist in South Dakota [who] surreptitiously records all incoming calls on his personal telephone, some of which come from out of state—specifically, he has recorded incoming calls from California, Illinois, and Wisconsin"—all for the sole purpose of gathering "telephonic speech data." You rule that the linguist's recording activities, even those involving interstate calls, would "probably" be allowed: "That some of the calls originated in California and Illinois—both of which are states that prohibit one-party consensual recording—is probably immaterial (though this question would ultimately have to be settled in the courts), given that the recording occurred in South Dakota and the case would be tried under federal law." Have the courts made any pertinent decisions?

ANSWER. Yes. In *Jewelcor v. Pre-Fab Panelwall, Inc.*, the Pennsylvania Superior Court held that where conversations occur between people located in different states, Title III preempts state law (though keep in mind that courts are by no means bound to follow one another's precedents). The following question and answer may also be of interest.

QUESTION. If a "listening device" is located in one jurisdiction, but the device's receiver is located in another, does "interception" then occur in the latter jurisdiction?

ANSWER. No. It has been established that interception, as it relates to aural acquisition, occurs in the jurisdiction where the listening device is located, regardless of the location of the receiver or the person using the device (*U.S. v. Nelson*).

QUESTION. If a linguist obtains someone's permission to surreptitiously record various conversations in which that person is a participant, but the person later decides to sue the linguist for invasion of privacy, would the linguist have to prove consent had been obtained?

ANSWER. Probably so. The available case law on determining the validity of consent to record surreptitiously uniformly involves situations in which the government was collecting evidence against an alleged criminal, but in the vast majority of those trials, as Carr (1991–92, 3: 95–96; see also 3: 96.1–104) states, "[t]he government [had] the burden of proving that consent was obtained from the consenting party" (see, for example, *U.S. v. Napier* and *People v. Patrick*; but cf. also *U.S. v. Ruppel*, in which the burden of proof was placed on the defendant to show the unlawfulness of the recording). It may also be worth noting that "voluntary" consent has been ruled to be coercion (and thus invalid) if the person granting the consent was rushed to make a decision (*State v. Dimeo*) or was so nervous when the permission was granted that she had not thoroughly read the consent form and had thus signed in the wrong place (*State v. Jones*). If, however, a linguist is sued for illegally recording or intercepting conversations (that is, if the issue is not consent, but legality), the burden of proof remains with the plaintiff (*Kassap v. Seitz*).

QUESTION. If a person whose conversations had been illegally recorded dies before the civil suit that he or she had filed is settled, can survivors continue the cause of action?

ANSWER. No. According to the ruling in *Pine v. Rust*, a cause of action brought under §2020 of Title III does not survive the plaintiff's death.

QUESTION. Are the "human subjects guidelines" that Donald W. Larmouth (1992) discusses legally binding?

ANSWER. Strictly speaking, no. The guidelines for research involving human subjects that Larmouth discusses in his essay cannot be enforced by prosecution and trial (because while they are based on federal POLICIES, as Larmouth points out, they are not grounded in federal STATUTES); but since linguists affiliated with colleges and universities usually sign contracts in which they promise to abide by all the "rules, regulations, and policies" of their institutions, noncompliance with any of those rules, regulations, or policies could result in disciplinary action (the worst-case scenario of which might result in termination of employment).

Several related points are salient here, however. First, we believe (unlike Larmouth, 7) that some legally recordable speech—for example, conversations in public places, in which the linguist does not know any of his or her informants—falls under the heading "public behavior," and so would be exempt from human subjects guidelines, even in spite of certain exceptions that invalidate the exemption. (According to the *Federal Policy for the Protection of Human Subjects; Notices and Rules* [28012], ratified on 18 June 1991, the exemption of "public behavior" is invalidated if "[i]nformation obtained is recorded in such a manner that human subjects can be identified, directly or through identifiers linked to the subjects"; and "any disclosure of the human subjects' responses outside the research could reasonably place the subjects at risk of criminal or civil liability or be damaging to the subjects' financial standing, employability, or reputation." Many colleges and universities add a third invalidation clause that proscribes the research from dealing with such "sensitive aspects of the subject's own behavior" as drug abuse, sexual behavior, or illegal conduct.)

Second, as Larmouth (12, 13) discusses, all legally recordable speech is exempted from human subjects guidelines if the informants are made aware (after the fact) that they have been recorded, and we endorse this procedure wholeheartedly. Again according to the *Federal Policy for the Protection of Human Subjects; Notices and Rules* (28016–17), such "awareness" must consist of full disclosure to the informants of the nature and purpose of the research, and must conclude with the informants giving their "uncoerced," "informed consent" for the data to be used (alternatively, the informants may request that the data be erased or otherwise destroyed). We will also point out that when we consulted with Kansas State University's attorneys, Office of Research and Sponsored Programs, and the committee responsible for the institution's *Handbook for Research, Demonstration or Other Activities Involving Human Subjects*, all admitted that the issue of surreptitious recording had not arisen before or, indeed, even been contemplated. When pushed for information, however, all maintained that (legal) surreptitious recording could be defended by the provisions of the *Handbook* as we have outlined here.

Third, we must wonder how strictly human subjects guidelines should be enforced. If the answer is that of course they should be enforced as strictly as possible, then much excellent data already gathered through surreptitious means would be tainted (see *PADS* 76, 50–53); but if the answer is that they should be enforced only sometimes, under only certain conditions, and that elsewhere they should be forgiven, then that line, however random, must be drawn with all due speed.

Finally, although we do not advocate anyone disobeying rules and regulations that he or she has contracted to obey, we are compelled to point out that university policies, like the policies of any business or institution (or, indeed, like the laws of any given jurisdiction), are only as strict as officials make them through monitoring and enforcement.

QUESTION. In his review of *PADS 76* (1993), Roger Shuy faults your synopsis of the history of legislation and jurisprudence affecting surreptitious recording. He writes: "It is difficult to imagine how the lawyer half of the authorial team managed to overlook the RICO Act of 15 October 1970 as a major contribution to surreptitious taping by law-enforcement agencies" (105). What is the RICO Act? How important is it? Is it pertinent to linguists?

ANSWER. The RICO (Racketeer Influenced Corrupt Organizations) Act, which appears as Title IX of the Organized Crime Control Act of 1970 (Pub. L. 91-452, 84 Stat. 941), was primarily concerned with how income derived from various racketeering activities—including murder, kidnapping, gambling, robbery, bribery, extortion, pornography, narcotics, and arson—could be invested in enterprises involved with or affecting interstate and foreign commerce. Its only commentary on surreptitious recording concerns those racketeering activities for which the interception of communications by law enforcement authorities is permitted. Contrary to Shuy's statement, neither of us "overlooked" the RICO Act; indeed, because it affects not one bit the legality of surreptitious recording by linguists who are "not acting under color of law," we consciously decided to exclude it from our review.

QUESTION. In *PADS 76*, as you advanced your argument for the prudent use of surreptitious recording as a means of gathering speech data, you noted that the practice has a time-honored history of use in many disciplines, including anthropology, speech pathology, sociology, and psycholinguistics. Why, as Roger Shuy noted in his review of the monograph (1993, 105–06), did you not also consider its "time-honored history of use" by various kinds of government-controlled organizations?

ANSWER. As we pointed out several times in *PADS 76*, our interest was—and remains—not in the government's multifaceted uses of surreptitious recording, all of which are regulated by a separate set of laws (and perhaps also ethics?) from those that govern private citizens; and certainly not in the linguistic analysis of government-authorized tape-recordings for the courtroom, whether those recordings were acquired surreptitiously or otherwise; but merely in the use of surreptitious recording by linguists as a means of gathering speech data.

QUESTION. Is it true, as Roger Shuy says in his review of *PADS 76* (1993, 104–05), that in 1978 the Linguistic Society of America, under the leadership of then-president William Labov, decided that the use of surreptitious recording as a means of gathering speech data was unethical?

ANSWER. To our knowledge the Linguistic Society of America (LSA) has never made any decision or issued any statement related directly to the use of surreptitious recording as a field technique. Shuy cites the 1978 annual report of the LSA's Executive Committee as evidence of such a decision, but when we queried Ms. Margaret Reynolds, LSA's Executive Director, she told us that while "[p]resident Labov did appoint a committee to address the topic of surreptitious recording . . . the committee did not file a final report" (personal communication, 31 March 1995).

Ms. Reynolds also told us that in May 1992 the Executive Committee approved a general policy statement on research involving human subjects (see the *LSA Bulletin*, no. 137 [October]). On reading that statement, however, we find that it comes no closer to discussing the topic of surreptitious recording than to note that linguistic research "must be conducted with respect for those who participate, with sensitivity as to their well being, and with concern for consequences of publication or sharing of results." We agree completely, and, contrary to Shuy's assertion, believe that nothing in these guidelines prohibits the judicious use of legal surreptitious recording as a field technique.

QUESTION. In his review of *PADS 76* (1993, 103), Roger Shuy faults Donald Larmouth for alleging that surreptitious recording is "probably representative of a great deal of linguistic fieldwork" (Larmouth 1992, 9) but offering no evidence to support that allegation. From the responses you have received to *PADS 76*, can you gauge how prevalent surreptitious recording is among linguists and what the consensus is toward the practice?

ANSWER. First we must note that Shuy misunderstood Larmouth's assertion. The language quoted above follows Larmouth's description of a hypothetical situation in which a dialect investigator, while gathering data through an interview with an informant, uses a concealed microphone to record everything the informant says, thus: "In this case, which is probably representative of a great deal of linguistic fieldwork, the use of a hidden microphone would appear to compromise the principle of informed consent" (9). The misunderstanding arises from the ambiguous antedecent of the phrase *this case*, which Larmouth intended to refer only to the scenario of a one-on-one interview being used to collect data on dialect, but which Shuy interpreted to mean the scenario of a one-on-one interview being used to collect data with a concealed microphone. The point Larmouth was trying to make was that if a hidden microphone were used in such a situation, APA guidelines for informed consent, risk, and deception would indicate that the informant ought to be debriefed (personal communication, 6 December 1994).

That aside, we begin our answer to the question with two caveats: First, only slightly more than 10% of the ADS membership responded to *PADS 76*, and only about 5% more responded orally or by e-mail. Second, many ADS members may not work with natural speech data, and thus have no intrinsic interest in field methodology or, more specifically, in surreptitious data collection; and, conversely, many field linguists who collect and analyze speech data regularly are not members of ADS. We cannot guess how many people fall into each of these categories; regarding the latter, however, Professor Edward Callary (Department of English, Northern Illinois University) wrote on 19 May 1992, shortly after the publication of *PADS 76*, that "many" subscribers to the electronic bulletin board LINGUIST had been speculating about the legality of various forms of surreptitious data collection, and that he had to make them aware of the existence of *PADS 76.*

These caveats in mind, the vast majority of our correspondents indicated either that they had recorded and/or continue to record at least some of their data surreptitiously, or that they believe surreptitious recording to be ethically justifiable in the context of acquiring objective linguistic data. Professor Leonard R. N. Ashley (Department of English, Brooklyn College, CUNY, in a letter dated 18 February 1994, summed up quite well the sentiment expressed most often: "My personal feeling is that what one says in public is recordable with or without the consent of the speaker," though the person recorded "owns the speech" and the researcher should be absolutely certain to use judiciously that which he or she has acquired. And Professor Timothy Frazer (Department of English, Western Illinois University) noted in a letter dated 17 May 1992 that he "[didn't] see any way around [the use of surreptitious recording] if we want untainted data."

Interestingly, Shuy never engages our observation in *PADS 76* that linguists have been recording data surreptitiously for decades except to note that, for him, our comment was a cheap shot in "the us/them theater of the dialectologists versus the sociolinguists" (104). We wish to make it clear that we intended nothing of the kind. Our only goal was to point out that while the technique of surreptitious recording has been and continues to be used a great deal by linguists, that use is too rarely discussed openly. Shuy also accuses us of making "a last, rear-guard dig at one of the experimental field techniques used by William Labov" (104). Again, we intended nothing of the kind. The fact remains, however, that Labov and hundreds of other linguists HAVE recorded surreptitiously, "experimentally" or not, and that such recording HAS often been facilitated by one kind of trick or another (such as when an informant is led to believe that a tape recorder has been turned off when in fact it is still running).

We might also add that linguists who work in academia frequently report that they are being asked to sanction student projects in which surreptitious recording is either necessary or desirable.

One typical example, reported by Professor Lise Winer (Department of Linguistics, Southern Illinois University at Carbondale) in a letter dated 2 April 1994, involved a graduate student who "wanted to do a study of authentic language of requests, in order to compare the results with what is offered in ESL textbooks." After securing Professor Winer's permission, and after pinpointing the university library's information and reference desks as two good locations for the collection of data, and after being authorized by the university's Human Subjects Committee (HSC) to tape-record surreptitiously (as part of the agreement, the student guaranteed her informants' anonymity and promised that all tapes would be erased at the conclusion of the study), AND after receiving support from the library's Director of Undergraduate and Institutional Services, the student was ultimately denied permission by the Dean of Library Affairs. The Dean's reasons, outlined in a letter dated 22 September 1993 and written to the student by the same Director of Undergraduate and Institutional Services who had earlier endorsed the project, were "that audio-recordings of patrons' requests might interfere with the normal operations of service counters and may possibly intimidate people who approach information desks."

What followed was truly a bureaucratic nightmare for everyone involved: Professor Winer, on behalf of the student, appealed the Dean's decision to the university's Graduate Council. Then, before the Council could respond, the Dean apparently rethought her position on the matter and agreed to abide by whatever judgment the HSC might render after reconsidering the entire case. Finally, when the HSC again decided in the student's favor, she was allowed to carry out her research—though more than six months had passed since the original decision of the HSC.

The Chairperson of the HSC, in his final memorandum on the matter (written to the Dean of Library Affairs and dated 10 November 1993, with copies, at this point, having to be sent not just to Professor Winer, but to the Chair of the Department of Linguistics, the Ombud, the Dean of the College of Liberal Arts, the Chair of the Graduate Council, the Director of the Office of Research Development and Administration, the Vice President for Academic Affairs and Provost, the Chair of the Graduate Council

Research Committee, and the Dean of the Graduate School), made some interesting points that are worth quoting at length:

> The Human Subjects Committee is primarily concerned with protecting the rights and welfare of human research subjects. Thus, we considered only the ethical issues surrounding the observation and recording for research purposes of requests for service made at library counters.... With regard to the ethical issue, we considered the behavior under observation to be "public" in that, from our experience, it is reasonable to assume that a conversation will be overhead [sic; read "overheard"] in that situation. Further, no record will be kept of either the identity of the individual[s] or the content[s] of the request[s]. Thus, there are no apparent risks to the subject[s].... I respect and appreciate your professional sensitivity to the privacy rights of library patrons.... I do not feel that the research in question compromises those rights....

In concluding this section, we would like to reiterate two brief points that we made in *PADS 76*. First, Title III and its various state correlates were drafted with law enforcement officials, not linguists, in mind. Even §2811[2][d], which governs activities done "not under color of law," was intended to clarify how government officials could gather evidence by using informants. Second, in all the case law—both federal and state—on the surreptitious interception and/or recording of communications, no linguist appears as a defendant even once (at least not in the capacity of field researcher). What all this means is that while our answers to the above questions are based on available statutes and judicial precedents, they should not necessarily be regarded as definitive.

VI. The Legality of Surreptitious Recording in Canada

The subject of surreptitious recording has become as complex in Canada as it is in the United States, and a comprehensive report—even one limited in scope to people not working for the government—would fill many more pages than we can reasonably allow. Our goal here, therefore, is merely to cover the essential points of the law and to provide sufficient references so that interested readers can easily investigate further on their own.

The history of the legality of surreptitious recording in Canada parallels that of the United States in many ways. Indeed, before

Parliament passed the Protection of Privacy Act (PPA) in 1974 (S.C. 1973–74, c. 50), no enforced legislation existed at the national level. (We write "enforced" because one statute did exist prior to the PPA, but was apparently never used [MacDonald 1987, 143]. Section 25 of An Act to Incorporate the Bell Telephone Company of Canada [S.C. 1880, c-67] warned that "[a]ny person who shall willfully or maliciously injure, molest or destroy any of the lines, posts or property of the Company, or in any way willfully obstruct or interfere with the working of the said telephone lines, and intercept any message transmitted thereon shall be guilty of a misdemeanor.") This is not to suggest that eavesdropping—and, later, wiretapping and bugging—had not been a problem in Canada; in fact, the cases filed between 1918 (perhaps the earliest, at least in this century) and the mid-1970s are numerous enough to conclude that a great deal of surreptitious listening and/or recording were being practiced, both by private citizens and by various law enforcement agencies (see, for example, *R. v. Mason, The King v. County of London Quarter Sessions Appeals Committee, Ex Parte Metropolitan Police Commissioner,* and *In Re Copeland and Adamson*). But the courts were forced to rule, in each of these cases, that no common law offense had been committed and that Canadians had no guaranteed right to privacy.

In 1964 Quebec passed the first provincial legislation concerning linguistic privacy (the Telegraph and Telephone Companies Act, R.S.Q. 1964, c. 286, §§22–24), which specifically prohibited anyone "from listening to or acquiring knowledge of conversations or messages passing over the lines of a telephone system" (Watt 1979, 25), but which also exempted from liability police officers acting in the line of duty. Following that model, five other provinces passed similar legislation during the remainder of the 1960s and in the early 1970s, always with the same exemption. In British Columbia, the Privacy Act (1968 [B.C.], c. 39) provides that it is tortious for anyone to willfully violate the privacy of another, and specifically mentions eavesdropping and surveillance—"whether or not accompanied by trespass"—as forbidden activities. The Government Telephones Act (R.S.A. 1970, c. 12, as amended) protects citizens of Alberta from illegal telephonic wiretapping and eavesdropping. The Privacy Act, 1974 (1973–74 [Sask.], c. 80), makes it tortious for anyone in Saskatchewan to "wilfully and without claim of right" violate the privacy of another, and includes all means of "auditory or visual" surveillance within its parameters. In Manitoba, two statutes protect the conversational privacy of citizens: the Telephone Act (R.S.M. 1970, c. T 40, as amended by 1977 [Man.], c. 45) prohibits telephonic wiretapping and recording; the Privacy Act (1970 [Man.], c. 74) makes it tortious for anyone to "substantially, unreasonably and without claim of right" violate the privacy of another person, and specifically forbids both auditory and visual surveillance. And the Telephone Act (R.S.O. 1970, c. 457) protects residents of Ontario from all forms of illegal telephonic wiretapping and recording. For further information on any of these statutes, see Watt (1979, 17–25).

The exemption of police officers was soon invoked to the point of abuse, however; indeed, MacDonald (1987, 144; footnotes omitted) says that

> [u]sually the only bodies regulating police wiretapping activities were the provincial Police Commissions who set guidelines for electronic surveillance. This required that the officer had reasonable and probable grounds for conducting a wiretap and that the Chief of Police gave his permission.... Hence, we had a situation where the police were policing themselves. Sometimes officers would act on their own initiative without informing or getting approval of those in command. This was discovered by the McDonald Commission's investigation into R.C.M.P. activities. [The McDonald Commission was one of several committees empowered by Parliament in the late 1960s and early 1970s to investigate police abuse of electronic surveillance.] The Royal Canadian Mounted Police officially maintained a policy against wiretapping yet nevertheless it went on. It appears that any controls maintained were very slack.

MacDonald also notes that "telephone companies cooperated with law enforcement agencies in tapping telephone lines" (144).

Because of this widespread abuse, the House of Commons Standing Committee on Justice and Legal Affairs soon recommended that—in general—"[w]iretapping and electronic eavesdropping should be made criminal offenses," and that law enforcement personnel should be allowed to use such methods in their work only with strict guidelines (Minutes and Proceedings of the Standing Committee on Justice and Legal Affairs [February 5,

1970, 2nd session, 28th Parliament], No. 7, 7). These recommendations eventually led to the adoption of the PPA, which came into effect on 30 June 1974, and was subsequently amended by §§7–12 of the Criminal Law Amendment Act in 1977 (S.C. 1976–77, c. 53).

Although the PPA effectively rewrote parts of the Criminal Code, the Crown Liability Act, and the Official Secrets Act (R.S.C. 1970, c. C-34, c. C-38, and c. 0-3, respectively, all as amended), we need consider here only its revisions to the Criminal Code (the Crown Liability Act governs how and by whom civil liability may be imposed on the Crown for infractions committed by "Crown servants"; the Official Secrets Act governs what may be done by the Solicitor General and others in the interest of national security). Part IV.I of the Code now prohibits the willful interception of a private communication by means of an electromagnetic, acoustic, mechanical, or other device (§178.11; as we shall see below, however, §§178.11(2)(a) and 178.11(3) specifically allow one-party consensual recording); the possession, sale, or purchase of such devices with the knowledge that they are designed for interception of private communications (§178.18); and the disclosure of information intercepted by means of such devices without the consent of the "object of the interception" (§178.20). (Each of these offenses allows for the exemption of law enforcement personnel provided that certain strict procedures are followed and limitations observed. We will not discuss these procedures and limitations; interested readers are referred to MacDonald [1987, 146].) The maximum penalty for these offenses is five years in the case of willful interception, and two years otherwise. The electronic devices used may also be forfeited (§178.19), and the court may, "upon the application of a person aggrieved," award up to $5,000 in punitive damages (§178.21).

Interested readers can find the complete text of Part IV.I in Watt 1983 (app. D, 103–60), where it is compared to the United States Title III, on which it was modeled. Here we wish to make the important point, following Watt (1979, 1; footnote omitted), that

[a]part from decisions which are grounded upon constitutional differences between . . . [Canada and the United States], the striking similarities in . . . [Part IV.1

and Title III] render invaluable the considered opinions of American courts upon questions which are either identical or similar to those which fail to be determined in accordance with the Canadian legislation.

Such was the finding in the landmark case of *R. v. Welsh and Ianuzzi (No. 6)*.

As with Title III, all of the potentially ambiguous terms in Part IV.1 have been meticulously defined elsewhere in the legislation (and, as MacDonald 1987, 155, notes, "if the surveillance activity does not fall within the definitions . . . then the provisions of Part IV.I do not apply"). In the following subsections, we present a synopsis of the most important of these definitions and their interpretations; for further information, including a plethora of judicial rulings (nearly all, however, centering on law enforcement personnel in their pursuit of alleged criminals), see Watt (1979, 27–65; 1983, 3–30) and MacDonald (1987).

§178.1 [PRIVATE COMMUNICATION]

A private communication is "any oral communication or any telecommunication made under circumstances in which it is reasonable for the originator thereof to expect that it will not be intercepted by any person other than the person intended by the originator thereof to receive it." Although the word *telecommunication* may seem vague here, the Interpretation Act (R.S.C. 1970, c. I-23) defines it quite comprehensively as "any transmission, emission or reception of signs, signals, writing, images or sounds or intelligence of any nature by wire, radio, visual or other electromagnetic system." The same section of the Act defines *radio* and *writing* just as broadly, leading one to conclude that the writers of the PPA intended all forms and kinds of communication to be protected from illegal surveillance.

Watt (1979, 28) explains that under this statute the level of privacy attached to a communication actually hinges on the courts' interpretation of *reasonable*, and that this interpretation is most heavily affected by the circumstances surrounding the communication:

It would seem obvious that statements uttered for public consumption in a public forum, or open to public officials would provide the clearest example of a statement beyond the reach of Part IV.I. Equally, in relation to the subjective expectation of privacy, a communicant who chooses a method of communication which exposes his statements to uninvited ears can scarcely assert a reasonable expectation of privacy in response to his implicit invitation to listen. Absent circumstances negating the subjective expectation of privacy of the originator of the statements, the inquiry then shifts to the reasonable expectation of privacy, a matter of inference in light of all relevant facts and circumstances. Relevant considerations include the location, content and purpose of the communication, the means by which it is transmitted, and the nature of the means, or techniques, if any, employed by the originator to prevent being overheard.

The "originator" of a communication has been found to be, for example, the person making the telephone call (*R. v. Miller et al.*) or the person speaking first in a face-to-face conversation, *unless* that person is a law enforcement officer who begins the conversation for the explicit purpose of gathering evidence (*R. v. Goldman*).

§178.1 [INTERCEPTION]

An interception is the act of someone "listen[ing] to, record[ing] or acquir[ing] a communication or acquir[ing] the substance, meaning or purport thereof." But when does an interception actually occur? If a telephone call intended for Person A is actually answered by Person B, for example, and the caller, unaware of whom he or she is speaking to, inadvertently divulges damaging or otherwise private information to Person B, has Person B "intercepted" the communication? In *R. v. McQueen*, the appeals court answered negatively, opining that since no interference had occurred between the origin of the call and its destination, there could have been no interception. That the caller was mistaken as to the identity of the receiver was, said the judge, irrelevant. On the other hand, the court ruled in *R. v. Dunn* that a person listening in on an extension telephone, even having the consent of the recipient of the call, has intercepted the call if the caller did not expect that third person to be on the line. Clearly the definition of *interception* is open to considerable interpretation.

§178.1 [ELECTROMAGNETIC, ACOUSTIC, MECHANICAL OR OTHER DEVICE]

The equipment defined by this statute includes "any device or apparatus that is used or is capable of being used to intercept a private communication, but does not include a hearing aid used to correct subnormal hearing of the user to not better than normal hearing." This language appears to be quite straightforward, but the courts have had some difficulty in interpreting it. It has been held, for example, that although a telephone is not such a device (*R. v. McQueen*), an extension telephone is (*R. v. Dunn*). Cellular phones are probably not "devices" under this statute, but the courts seem not yet to have debated the issue (the pressure is mounting, however; see Brady and Quinn 1990).

And what of video equipment? The trial judge in *R. v. Irwin and Sansone et al.* rejected evidence that had been collected using a closed circuit camera, but the appeals court reversed the lower decision (though on the basis that the evidence had been collected before the statute had been passed, all the while remaining silent on the issue of whether video cameras are "devices" under this statute). A different appeals court (with the Supreme Court later concurring), in *R. v. Wong*, also circumvented the issue by holding that regardless of whether video cameras are "devices," their surreptitious use violates §8 of the Canadian Charter of Rights and Freedoms (Part I of the Constitution Act 1982 [Schedule B of the Canada Act 1982], [U.K.], 1982, c. 11). The Supreme Court has yet to rule on a precise, explicit definition of "electromagnetic, acoustic, mechanical or other device."

§§178.11[2][A] AND [3] [ONE-PARTY CONSENSUAL SURVEILLANCE]

As mentioned earlier, one-party consensual recording is generally allowed, and these statutes specify under what conditions. Section 178.11(2)(a) frees from liability any person 'who has the consent to intercept, express or implied, of the originator of the private communication or of the person intended by the originator thereof to receive it"; §178.11 (3) states that "[w]here a private communication is originated by more than one person or is intended by the originator thereof to be received by more than one person, a consent to the interception thereof by any one of such persons is sufficient [to relieve the interceptor from liability for interception and/or eventual use and/or disclosure]." As in the United States, the consent must be given freely and without coercion (*R. v. Goldman, R. v. Rosen*), and is necessary for surreptitious recordings to be admitted into evidence in a trial (that is, illegally gained recordings can be suppressed; see §178.16). As MacDonald (1987, 155) rightfully concludes, "[h]aving the consent of one of the parties turns what otherwise would be an illegal activity into a legal one."

The future of surreptitious recording in Canada can be described only as extremely uncertain. In 1990 the Supreme Court, in a landmark case, ruled that one-party consensual recording (audio as well as video) violates the Canadian Charter when used by law enforcement personnel to gather evidence (*R. v. Duarte*). As Rabideau (1991, 176) explains, the Court "determined that there was no logical distinction between participant and third party surveillance"; that the option to use one-party consensual recording "gave the state unfettered discretion to record communications notwithstanding the consent of one of the parties"; and that such recording "was therefore a significant infringement of the s. 8 right to privacy" guaranteed by the Charter.

In the years since *R. v. Duarte*, the precedent set there has been followed by courts at every level all across the country in literally dozens of cases (see, for example, *R. v. Wiggins, R. v. F. (H.), R. v. Greffe, R. v. Wile, R. v. Thompson, R. v. Kokesch, R. v. Wong, R. v. Garofoli, R. v. Montoute, R. v. Barnes, R. v. Rodney, R. v. Spennato, R. v. Blackmore et al., R. v. Aranda, R. v. Wills, Canadian Civil Liberties Union v. Canada, R. v. Clymore, R. v. Fegan, R. v. Tam, R. v. Elzein, R. v. Sandhu, R. v. Solomon, R. v. Giesecke, R. v. Unger, R. v. Plant, R. v. Grant, R. v. Smyk, R. v. Bisson,* and *R. v. Wijesinha*), thus making it extremely difficult for judges to dissent in the future. Nevertheless, these rulings apply only to investigations done by the state; "[t]he decision[s have] absolutely no effect on participant surveillance carried out by private individuals" (Rabideau 1991, 184). It seems unlikely, however, that Canada will long endure a situation in which ordinary citizens have the right to gather information using methods that have been explicitly forbidden from governmental use. The scales of privacy have been tipped too far in one direction; to balance them, either the Supreme Court will strike down the use of one-party consensual recording by private citizens as unconstitutional or Parliament will pass new legislation re-empowering provincial officials. In either case, our advice to linguists who record surreptitiously in Canada is to proceed cautiously and with one eye on Parliament and the Supreme Court at all times.

VII. The Legality of Surreptitious Video Recording

Following the publication of *PADS 76*, a number of colleagues wrote to us asking for guidance regarding the legality of surreptitious VIDEO recording. This is a topic that had occurred to us in 1988, as we were doing our original research, but one that we ultimately decided to omit from our discussion, believing that not many linguists would be interested. We were evidently mistaken: besides those sociolinguists who incorporate visually acquired data into their analyses of speech, apparently many linguists are interested specifically in the roles kinesics, proxemics, and haptics play in the communication process. Certainly all these scholars (whom one colleague referred to as "etholinguists") have as great a need for recording good field data as the rest of us; thus the inclusion of this section.

Although surreptitious video recording is obviously more intrusive on an individual's privacy than any kind of aural eavesdropping, it is not currently subject to any specific federal or state legislation—and, as many legal scholars have pointed out, this lack of such statutory control constitutes yet another example of Congress lagging far behind technology.

(Readers unfamiliar with the sophistication of recent advances in video surveillance may be interested in the remarks of Greenfield [1991, 1047–48; numerous footnotes are omitted]:

The nature of E[lectronic] V[ideo] S[urveillance] allows privacy to be infringed absolutely. [¶] ... Miniature video cameras readily available on the retail market weigh less than two pounds and can fit in the palm of one's hand. These cameras can easily be concealed in a briefcase, a lamp, a plant, a lunch box, a television, or even a teddy bear. Miniature cameras can be disguised as cigarette lighters or watches. Moreover, special lenses can make a camera even more secret. A camera fitted with a "pinhole lens" is virtually undetectable because the aperture of its conical lens has a diameter of less than ⅛ of an inch. Cameras equipped with such lenses can be hidden in sprinkler heads, heating vents, or even clocks. [¶] ... Pocket-sized infrared cameras [that can capture detailed, high-resolution visual images] are [also] available on the retail market. Furthermore, computer imaging systems can create images without having to "see" at all. Technicians can use sound waves or microwave technology to gather huge data sets, which computers can then transform into visual images.

For those who may be interested, the omitted footnotes list retail dealers, prices, and other purchasing information. There can be little doubt, too, that since Greenfield published his article, both eavesdropping technology and its availability have increased greatly.)

With the courts left at their own discretion to determine what is and is not lawful, at least three questions arise: First, is Title III, which was drafted specifically to delimit the legal bounds of surreptitious AUDIO recording, applicable to NON-audio recording as well? Second, can the Constitution—especially the Fourth Amendment, which regulates "unreasonable searches and seizures"—offer any guidance on the issue of what is allowable and what is not? And finally, can the numerous judicial rulings in cases involving eavesdropping and audio surveillance be brought to bear as precedents? As we shall see, the courts have been wrestling with these difficult questions for nearly three decades, and as might be expected, definite answers have been slow to emerge.

In 1989, the First Circuit Court of Appeals held that Title III applied to video as well as audio recordings (*U.S. v. Bernal*), thus setting an important precedent. Over the next few years, however, that precedent was ignored as four different Circuit Courts ruled that Title III regulated "only the interception of wire and oral communications" (*U.S. v. Torres, U.S. v. Biasucci, U.S. v. Cuevas-Sanchez,* and *U.S. v. Mesa-Rincon*), and that therefore "the use of video equipment [was] not covered by the statute where only a video record [was] created, used, or disclosed" (Carr 1991–92, 3: 119).

As with so many aspects of the law, of course, the situation was not as clearcut as these comments would have it seem. Citing §2511(2)(d) of Title III (which, recall, discusses only "wire, oral, or electronic" communications), one federal court had ruled as early as 1972 that a "tortious act" could be committed with a camera (*Galella v. Onassis*). Moreover, according to the legislative history of §2510(12) and (13), which discuss the definitions of *electronic communication* and *user* (of a device to intercept wire, oral, or electronic communications), respectively (see H. Rep. No. 99-647), if a person or "entity" transmits by any method a closed-circuit television picture of a meeting, that transmission is protected under Title III. And, of course, if video equipment records oral communications as well as visual images, Title III would apply to the audio portion of the videotape (*People v. Teicher, Boddie v. American Broadcasting Co. (1)*; but cf. also *U.S. v. Pageau*).

Late in 1991, the Ninth Circuit opined that federal law enforcement officials *are* constrained by Title III in their use of video equipment, since that statute was intended to govern "all highly intrusive forms of surveillance" (*U.S. v. Koyomejian* at 1451; see also Carrizosa 1991). With such diametrically opposed opinions now recorded by the judiciaries of several peer Circuits, the matter can only be resolved by the Supreme Court. In the meantime, rulings of the lower courts on similar cases are unpredictable. (In 1993, to cite just one instance, a United States District Court, following the opinion rendered in *U.S. v. Bernal*, held that "[t]he standard of review applicable to audio tape recordings applies to video recordings as well" [*U.S. v. Arriaga* at 1523].)

Thus is answered the first of the three questions posed above. And the others can be addressed just as quickly and, perhaps, a bit more definitively: the courts have held that the Fourth Amendment DOES apply to cases involving surreptitious video recording, and they HAVE relied heavily on judicial precedents from audio cases in reaching their decisions. Various examples of this application and these precedents will occupy us for most of the rest of this section.

For our purposes here, the central consideration in Fourth Amendment questions regarding the legality of surreptitious video recording centers on the term *search*. The Fourth Amendment states that

> The right of the people to be secure in their persons, houses, papers, and effects, against unreasonable searches and seizures, shall not be violated, and no Warrants shall issue, but upon probable cause, supported by Oath or affirmation, and particularly describing the place to be searched, and the persons or things to be seized.

As such, it offers protection only from GOVERNMENT searches; but as we have seen, judges have been integrating the conditions for Fourth Amendment privacy into their opinions involving Title III regularly since 1967, when *Katz v. U.S.* was decided. Our attention in this section to judicial precedents involving violations of Fourth Amendment rights is therefore not misplaced. (For an excellent overview of basic Fourth Amendment principles as they apply to the issue of surreptitious recording—audio or video—see Fishman 1988, 318–22.)

But what precisely constitutes a "search"? By and large, the courts have tried to adhere to the principles first established in *Katz v. U.S.*: first, that a search occurs when an individual's "reasonable expectation" of privacy has been violated; second, that this "expectation be one that society is prepared to recognize as 'reasonable'" (389 U.S. at 361). And as we have already seen repeatedly, this second principle is not at all straightforward. Indeed, as Scharrer (1989, 500) observes, "[a]lthough a person can take precautions to safeguard his privacy and therefore have a subjective expectation of privacy, taking precautions is irrelevant if that expectation is not reasonable. Reasonableness does not depend on whether the person is likely to be observed." It depends, instead, on whether an intrusion "infringes upon the personal societal values protected by the [F]ourth [A]mendment" (*Oliver v. U.S.* at 182). Thus in *McCray v. State*, for example, in which damning evidence had been acquired merely by filming the defendant walking across the street, an appellate court in Maryland ruled that no violation of the Fourth Amendment had occurred because society would not recognize walking on a public thoroughfare as "private" behavior.

The Supreme Court has not yet heard a case directly involving both the Fourth Amendment and surreptitious video recording. Nonetheless, since 1983 it has considered at least seven cases in which "decisions have focused at least in part upon application of the Fourth Amendment to technological enhancement of, or technological substitution for, visual surveillance" (Fishman 1988, 317; see *U.S. v. Dunn, Texas v. Brown, U.S. v. Knotts, U.S. v. Karo, California v. Ciraolo, Florida v. Riley*, and *Dow Chemical Co. v. U.S.*). And the Court has consistently focused on three issues in deciding when such technology constitutes a search: the extent to which the equipment enhanced its user's natural senses; the availability of such equipment to the general public; and the nature of the information sought or discovered by the surveillance. As Fishman (1988, 323) concludes, "[t]he more revealing and sense-enhancing . . . the equipment is, the more likely a court will consider . . . [its] use . . . to be a search. On the other hand, the more widely available a particular item of . . . equipment is, the less likely it is that its use will be considered a search." More information on each of these issues can be found in Fishman (1988), and see also Evans (1988); our point is merely that the same criteria, among others, will almost certainly surface again when the Supreme Court decides its first case involving the legality of surreptitious video recording.

Several of the Circuit Courts have decided cases concerning the Fourth Amendment as it relates to surreptitious video recording, as have several federal district courts—and as Greenfield (1991, 1057) explains, the general conclusion is that the practice is illegal if done "in nonpublic areas and without the consent of a person present." What constitutes a "nonpublic place"? The question has no definitive answer, of course, but to date such places have included homes (*Ricks v. State*), offices (*People v. Teicher* and *U.S. v. Taketa*), some fenced yards (depending on the kind of fence and its height; *U.S. v. Cuevas-Sanchez*), and some of the stalls in public restrooms (depending on where in the restroom the stalls are situated, whether the stalls have doors, what the person in the stall is doing, and so forth; *Smayda v. U.S., Commonwealth v. Bloom, State v. Limberhand,* and *People v. Dezek,* among many others). On the other hand, some courts have allowed surreptitious video recording even in "nonpublic" areas, but only on the consent of either "a person who has authority over the particular area" (Carr 1991–92, 3: 120; see *U.S. v. Laetividal-Gonzalez, People v. Winograd,* and *State v. Raymer*) or a person who is a party to the scene or event being recorded (*People v. Henderson, Benford v. American Broadcasting Co., Inc. et al.*; but cf. also *Commonwealth v. Kean,* in which the court held that the recording of sexual activities by one of the participants violated the right to privacy of the other participant).

The decision in *U.S. v. Taketa* is particularly interesting in what it says regarding an individual's right to privacy. The defendant had been videotaped in a colleague's office, but neither he nor that colleague was aware of the camera's presence. The unanimous ruling of the 9th Circuit Court of Appeals, written by Judge Robert R. Beezer, was that through subjective expectations, "persons may create temporary zones of privacy within which they may not be reasonably videotaped . . . [e]ven when that zone is a place they do not own or normally control, and in which they might not be able reasonably to challenge a search at some other time or by some other means. . ." (quoted in Cox 1991, 14).

Finally, although they do not yet seem to have played a role in judicial rulings involving surreptitious video recording, we should certainly discuss two terms relevant to the Fourth Amendment right to visual privacy—*open fields* and *plain view.* To begin, we cite the facts of *Oliver v. U.S.* as summarized by Evans (1988, 120; footnotes are omitted, but paraphrased in square brackets):

> . . . acting on a tip, [police officials] . . . walked a distance over one mile on the defendant's property past several obstructions [including a locked gate, several fences, and several "No Trespassing" signs] and discovered a well-hidden marijuana patch. [The patch was surrounded by woods, embankments, and fences, and could not be seen from any point of public access.] Having used the visual evidence collected from the trip to show probable cause, the police obtained a valid search warrant and prosecuted the defendant.

The Supreme Court ruled that no violation of the Fourth Amendment had occurred, thus affirming (and even quoting from) what has come to be known as the "open fields" doctrine: "the special protection accorded by the Fourth Amendment to the people in their 'persons, houses, papers, and effects,' is not extended to the open fields" (*Hester v. U.S.* at 59). And *open fields* has elsewhere been defined by the Court as an area not "so intimately tied to the home itself that it should be placed under the home's 'umbrella' of Fourth Amendment protection" (*U.S. v. Dunn* at 1139). In general, this area—a home's curtilage—is defined by four factors: (1) the proximity of the area to the home; (2) whether the area is enclosed by any structure that surrounds the home; (3) how the area is used by the home's occupants; and (4) whether the home's occupants have taken steps to protect the area from observation (*U.S. v. Dunn* at 1139). Everything not within a home's curtilage is considered "open fields" (*Hester v. U.S.*).

Whatever protection this notion of "curtilage" may afford, the Supreme Court has limited it by creating the "plain view" rule, which states simply that no "search" or "seizure" has occurred if a government official has merely observed things that a curious passerby might also observe (*James v. U.S.* at 1151, n. 1). This apparent loophole has allowed police officers to peek through a gap in closed garage doors (*U.S. v. Wright*), to see inside a barn by using a flashlight, all the while remaining outside the structure (*U.S. v. Dunn*), to observe below with binoculars while flying in a helicopter (*State v. Stachler*), to peer into a parked truck (*U.S. v. Arredondo-Hernandez*), to look through undrawn window curtains (*People v. Hicks*), and even to examine the contents of a room after having walked through a door that was blowing in the wind (*Jessee v. State*).

By way of concluding this section, we wish to make several specific recommendations to linguists who use surreptitious video recording as a means of collecting nonverbal data:

1. Record surreptitiously only to gain data that could not otherwise be obtained.

2. Proceed with extreme caution, and use common sense. With no specific federal or state legislation and a relative paucity of judicial precedents—some of which contradict one another—to guide them, the courts are establishing the law in this area with each case they hear.

3. Be aware that most courts seem to be guided by Title III, and will therefore almost certainly disallow nonconsensual recording in nonpublic areas.

4. Remember that the definition of *nonpublic* as it bears on a person's "expectation of privacy" and whether society is prepared to label that expectation "reasonable" is not at all well established, even considering the "open fields" doctrine and "plain view" rule. We would assume that areas such as shopping malls, public streets and sidewalks, public parks, and the like would be classified as generally "accessible to the public" (*Oliver v. U.S.* at 179), but, again, the courts decide each case on its own merits.

5. Use equipment that does not "enhance your senses" (as, for example, with a zoom lens or infrared lighting) and that is widely available on the retail market.

6. Be certain that your motive in recording is in no way tortious, criminal, or otherwise suspicious, for that fact alone will almost certainly render the recording illegal.

VIII. The Future of Surreptitious Recording

In this essay we have attempted to complement and enlarge upon what we wrote in *PADS 76* regarding the legality of surreptitious recording. Because we have intended the preceding sections to be self-contained discussions of the various topics considered, we will not summarize our conclusions here; instead, our final remarks will speculate on the future of surreptitious recording in the United States.

There is no question that federal legislation continues to lag behind the technology associated with surreptitious listening and recording (see, e.g., Moskowitz 1990 and Heredia 1992, 334, and note that the same is true of state legislation; in fact, some states still have no laws governing the practices)—and this in spite of the formation in 1987 of a Senate subcommittee "to ensure that American laws keep pace with new technologies" (Warren, Thorwaldson, and Koball 1991, 204–05). Indeed, some experts suggested in 1988 that the newly-passed ECPA was even then a decade behind the most recent advances in surveillance equipment (see Zuckerman 1988). Nor is this technology restricted to the black market, as one might suppose. In 1990, for example, private individuals in the United States collectively spent more than $200,000,000 on retail sales of eavesdropping equipment (see Lacayo 1991; that figure does not include the other millions of dollars spent on the kinds of surreptitious video recording equipment mentioned in section VII)—including parabolic microphones that can easily record conversations from more than half a mile away, pinhead-sized receivers with incredible aural sensitivity, virtually undetectable telephone-tapping devices, and even equipment to intercept the radio waves emitted by computers (thus enabling all computer work to be intercepted from more than a mile away). One might guess such equipment to be terribly expensive, but such is often not the case (see Stewart 1988), especially since numerous popular magazines regularly publish "how-to" articles describing how inexpensive parts available at any electronics store can be combined into relatively sophisticated equipment (according to Church 1987, for example, the equipment used to intercept a computer's radio waves could be assembled for less than $300 in 1987, and that price has almost certainly declined in the years since).

This Congressional lag causes the courts to be called on more and more often to establish judicial precedents, and the pattern of such precedents in the latter part of the twentieth century thus far has been one of increasing leniency. Kroll (1987, 72), for example, noted almost a decade ago that "the list of technological advances that threaten privacy is growing almost by the day, and the judicial acceptance of their use seems unabated." Similarly, Flaherty (1989, 315) says that the courts have developed "high standards . . . for proof of damages for invasion of privacy." And Stephens (1990, 22) notes that "[g]iven the direction of the [Supreme] Court, it may eventually adopt the maxim long held by many law-enforcement officers: If you have nothing to hide, you have nothing to fear." This tendency of the Supreme Court to limit individuals' rights to privacy has been noted and discussed by legal commentators for nearly a generation; see especially Brennan (1977), Silverstein (1982, 1989), and Reuben (1990).

This judicial trend, however, will almost certainly not go unchecked forever. As Americans become increasingly aware that their right to privacy is slowly eroding, Congress will have to act (cf. the remarks of Gutterman 1988 and Katz 1990). It has even been suggested that such action will come in the form of a constitutional amendment which would, in very specific language, limit the means by which one individual can invade the privacy of another. In fact, Laurence H. Tribe, now Professor of Constitutional Law at Harvard Law School and formerly a clerk for Supreme Court Justice Potter Stewart (author of the majority opinion in *Katz v. U.S.*), has proposed just such an amendment (see Warren, Thorwaldson, and Koball 1991, 12):

This Constitution's protections for the freedoms of speech, press, petition, and assembly, and its protections against unreasonable searches and seizures and the deprivation of life, liberty or property without due process of law, shall be construed as fully applicable without regard to the technological method or medium through which information content is generated, altered, transmitted or controlled.

This amendment, or one similar to it, would effectively end virtually all the now-legal surreptitious interception and recording done in the United States, whether through audio, video, or other means.

Ironically, Congress never intended for surreptitious recording to be as legal as it is. The legislative history of §2511(2)(d) clearly states that the Senate's intent in proposing the bill was *not* to legalize all non-tortious, non-criminal one-party consensual recording by people "not acting under color of law," but "to prohibit a one-party consent tap except for law enforcement officials, and for private persons who act in a defensive fashion" (114 Cong. Rec. 14694 [23 May 1968]). In other words, what was originally meant to exist only for certain restricted "proper" purposes is now widely used for all but the most "improper" of purposes. Why Congress never backtracked to correct itself and re-establish Title III as it was originally intended remains a mystery.

Meanwhile, surreptitious listening, looking, and/or recording remain viable methods by which linguists can gather data. Our continuing two-pronged advice for those who plan to use any such technique, however, is to stay abreast of the relevant federal and state legislation and case law, and to do what you do carefully, wisely, and with all due regard for your informants.

Notes

1. We will need to return to Shuy's review several times in Section V, but perhaps here is the best place to note for the record that we were very disappointed with it—not because it was negative, but because it was not carefully done. The general tone of that review and Shuy's frequent misreading of our article suggest that he really did not wish to review *PADS 76* as much as present his own view of linguists using surreptitious recording to gather speech data. Clearly he does not favor it.

2. This section summarizes pages 17–29 of the essay in *PADS 76*.

3. Although discussions of the ECPA are numerous in the legal literature, readable discussions are truly rare. For one of the best—and one that goes into much more detail than we provide either here or in *PADS 76*—see Kastenmeier, Leavy, and Beier (1989).

4. Each chapter of Carr's book begins its pagination anew, and incorporates the chapter number into the page number; thus the present citation, "3: 3," refers to chapter 3, page 3.

References Cited

Books and Articles

Atkinson, Leonard. 1991. "The Origins of Wiretapping in Connecticut." *University of Bridgeport Law Review* 12: 247–92.

Baumhart, Julia Turner. 1992. "The Employer's Right to Read Employee E-Mail: Protecting Property or Personal Prying?" *The Labor Lawyer* 8: 923–48.

Bindler, Susan Ellen. 1992. "Peek and Spy: A Proposal for Federal Regulation of Electronic Monitoring in the Work Place." *Washington University Law Quarterly* 70: 853–85.

Bowling, L. Roger. 1987. "Am. Sub. S.B. 222: Surveillance in Ohio." *University of Dayton Law Review* 13: 129–44.

Brady, Diane, and Hal Quinn. 1990. "Cellular Storm." *Mcclean's* 103 [30 July]: 40.

Brennan, William J., Jr. 1977. "State Constitutions and the Protection of Individual Rights." *Harvard Law Review* 90: 489–504.

Burnside, Russell S. 1987. "The Electronic Communications Privacy Act of 1986: The Challenge of Applying Ambiguous Statutory Language to Intricate Telecommunication Technologies." *Rutgers Computer and Technology Law Journal* 13: 451–517.

Carr, James G. 1987. "Privacy of Electronic Communications under Title III." *Search and Seizure Law Report* 14: 105–12.

———. 1991–92. *The Law of Electronic Surveillance*, 3rd ed. New York: Clark Boardman Callaghan.

Carrizosa, Philip. 1991. "Wiretap Rules Held Applicable in Use of Video." *The Los Angeles Daily Journal*, issue N 206 [16 Oct.]: 1-4.

Carter, Derrick A. 1991. "Distinguished Brief Award: *People of the State of Michigan v. W. C. Collins. Thomas M. Cooley Law Review* 8: 177–241.

Charles, Joel. Forthcoming. "Bibliography of Forensic Titles Pertaining to Sound Recordings." Audio Engineering Society.

Church, George J. 1987. "The Art of High Tech Snooping." *Time* 129 [20 Apr.]: 22–24.

Cinquegrana, Americo R. 1989. "The Walls (and Wires) Have Ears: The Background and First Ten Years of the Foreign Intelligence Act of 1978." *University of Pennsylvania Law Review* 137: 793–828.

Clukey, Laura L. 1988. "The Electronic Communications Privacy Act of 1986: The Impact on Software Communication Technologies." *Software Law Journal* 2: 243–63.

Cohen, Joel. 1989. "Consensual Recordings—A Primer on New York Law." *New York Law Journal* 201.5 [9 Jan.]: 1, 5–6.

Cox, Gail Diana. 1991. "9th Circuit Controls Official Video Power." *The National Law Journal* 20 [21 Jan.]: 14.

Elmer-Dewitt, Philip. 1994. "Battle for the Soul of the Internet." *Time* 144 [25 July]: 50–56.

Evans, Robert M., Jr. 1988. "Reasonable Expectations of Privacy and High Technology Surveillance: The Impact of *California v. Ciraolo* and *Dow Chemical v. U.S.* on Title III of the Omnibus Crime Control and Safe Streets Act." *Washington University Law Quarterly* 66: 111–33.

Federal Policy for the Protection of Human Subjects; Notices and Rules. 1991. Washington, D.C.: Department of Health and Human Services, Federal Register 56, 117 [16 June]: 28001–32.

Fishman, Clifford S. 1988. "Technologically Enhanced Visual Surveillance and the Fourth Amendment: Sophistication, Availability and the Expectation of Privacy." *American Criminal Law Review* 26: 315–58.

———. 1991. *Wiretapping and Eavesdropping* (Cumulative Supplement). Rochester, NY: Lawyers Co-operative Publishing Co.

Flaherty, David H. 1989. *Protecting Privacy in Surveillance Societies.* Chapel Hill: U of North Carolina P.

Gluck, Jon. 1994. "Technology Jane." *Self* Aug.: 24.
Goldsmith, Michael, and Kathryn Ogden Balmforth. 1991. "The Electronic Surveillance of Privileged Communications: A Conflict in Doctrines." *Southern California Law Review* 64: 903–50.
Greenfield, Kent. 1991. "Cameras in Teddy Bears: Electronic Visual Surveillance and the Fourth Amendment." *University of Chicago Law Review* 58: 1045–77.
Gutterman, Melvin. 1988. "A Formulation of the Value and Means Models of the Fourth Amendment in the Age of Technologically Enhanced Surveillance." *Syracuse Law Review* 39: 647–735.
Handbook for Research, Demonstration or Other Activities Involving Human Subjects. 1992. Faculty Handbook, Kansas State University.
Hendrick, Vincent J. X., II. 1988. "The Admissibility of Tape Recorded Evidence Produced by Private Individuals under Title III of the Omnibus Crime Control Act of 1968." *Washington and Lee Law Review* 45: 231–48.
Heredia, Hannibal F. 1992. "Is There Privacy in the Workplace?: Guaranteeing a Broader Privacy Right for Workers under California Law." *Southwestern University Law Review* 22: 307–35.
Hernandez, Ruel Torres. 1988. "ECPA and Online Computer Privacy." *Federal Communications Law Journal* 41: 17–41.
Jackson, James O. 1995. "It's a Wired, Wired World." *Time* 145 [Spring Special Issue]: 80–82.
Kastenmeier, Robert W., Deborah Leavy, and David Beier. 1989. "Communications Privacy: A Legislative Perspective." *Wisconsin Law Review* 1989: 715–37.
Katz, Lewis R. 1990. "In Search of a Fourth Amendment for the Twenty-First Century." *Indiana Law Journal* 65: 549–90.
Knowlton, Thomas A. 1988. "Interceptors and Innocent Recipients: Applying the Federal Wiretapping Law's Exclusionary Rule to Private Participant Monitoring." *Boston College Law Review* 29: 901–40.
Kopecky, Susan L. 1993. "Dealing with Intercepted Communications: Title III of the Omnibus Crime Control and Safe Streets Act in Civil Litigation." *The Review of Litigation* 12: 441–65.
Kroll, Robert E. 1987. "Can the Fourth Amendment Go High Tech?" *ABA Journal* 73 [1 Sept.]: 70–72, 74.
Lacayo, Richard. 1991. "Do-it-yourself Espionage." *Time* 138 [11 Nov.]: 38.
Larmouth, Donald W. 1992. "The Legal and Ethical Status of Surreptitious Recording in Dialect Research: Do Human Subjects Guidelines Apply?" *Publication of the American Dialect Society* 76: 1–14.
Licata, Lon A. 1988-89. "The End of Substantial Compliance with Nebraska's Wiretap Law?" *Creighton Law Review* 22: 475–96.
Loeb, Robert A. 1993. "Eavesdropping in Illinois: The Conflict Between Statutory and Case Law." *Illinois Bar Journal* 81: 16–18, 20–21, 43.

MacDonald, Norman. 1987. "Electronic Surveillance in Crime Detection: An Analysis of Canadian Wiretapping Law." *The Dalhousie Law Journal* 10: 141–66.

Marcus, Martin. 1988. "The New State Law on Eavesdropping and Other Forms of Surveillance." *New York Law Journal* 200 [3 Dec.]: 1, 7.

McAllister, Stephen R. 1995. "Practice Before the Supreme Court of the United States." *The Journal of the Kansas Bar Association* 64: 25–43.

Messana, Thomas M. 1989. "*Ricks v. State*: Big Brother Has Arrived in Maryland." *Maryland Law Review* 48: 435–54.

Meyer, Fred Jay. 1988. "Don't Touch That Dial: Radio Listening under the Electronic Communications Privacy Act of 1986." *New York University Law Review* 63: 416–48.

Moskowitz, Daniel B. 1990. "Electronic Mail Security Is Hot New Issue." *Washington Post* 22 Oct.: F35.

Murray, Thomas E. 1993. "Methods in Dialectology: Reappraising the 'State of the Art'; or, How to Be a 'Maverick Sociolinguist' without Really Trying." National meeting of the American Dialect Society. Toronto, Ontario, 28–30 Dec.

Murray, Thomas E., and Carmin Ross-Murray. 1992. "On the Legality and Ethics of Surreptitious Recording." *Publication of the American Dialect Society* 76: 15–75.

Pennypacker, Philip P. 1989. "Reach Out and Bug Someone: California's New Wiretap Law." *Santa Clara Law Review* 29: 275–99.

Rabideau, Monique. 1991. "*Duarte v. R.*: In Fear of Big Brother." *University of Toronto Faculty of Law Review* 49: 171–85.

Reed, Scott O. 1988. "Eavesdropping Regulation in Illinois." *The John Marshall Law Review* 21: 251–307.

Render, Edwin D., and Robert D. McClure. 1991. "A Recent Sixth Circuit Debate. Surreptitious Monitoring by a Participant in a Conversation: Does Title III Impose Liability Even if the Recording Is Never Divulged?" *University of Toledo Law Review* 22: 427–53.

Reuben, Richard C. 1990. "Privacy: The Issue of the '90s." *California Law* 10 [Mar.]: 38–42.

Richman, Steven M. 1987. "Voices that Go Bump in the Night: Conflicting Rights under the Wiretap Statutes." *Seton Hall Legislative Journal* 11: 171–99.

Robinson, Linda S. 1991. "Wrong Number: Disconnecting the Cordless Telephone from the Right to Privacy." *Criminal Justice Journal* 13: 101–14.

Sapp, Stephen L. 1989. "Private Interceptions of Wire and Oral Communications under Title III: Rethinking Congressional Intent." *American Journal of Criminal Law* 16: 181–205.

Scharrer, Jeanette R. 1989. "Covert Electronic Surveillance of Public Rest Rooms: Privacy in the Common Area?" *Cooley Law Review* 6: 495–510.

Shuy, Roger W. 1993. "Risk, Deception, Confidentiality, and Informed Consent" Review of *PADS 76: Legal and Ethical Issues in Surreptitious Recording. American Speech* 68: 103–06.

Silverstein, Mark. 1982. "Developments in the Law—The Misinterpretation of State Constitutional Rights." *Harvard Law Review* 95: 1324–1502.

———. 1989. "Privacy Rights in State Constitutions: Models for Illinois?" *University of Illinois Law Review* 1989: 215–96.

Smith, Thomas M. 1989. "The Suppression Sanction under the Electronic Communications Privacy Act for Violations of the Private One-party Consent Exception." *Villanova Law Review* 34: 111–43.

Stephens, Cori D. 1990. "All's Fair: No Remedy under Title III for Interspousal Surveillance." *Fordham Law Review* 57: 1035–52.

Stewart, Doug. 1988. "Spy Tech." *Discover* 9 [3 Mar.]: 58–65.

Strugatz, Michael D. 1990. "Criminal Procedure—Cordless Telephone Communications and the Federal Wiretap Act—*Tyler v. Berodt*, 877 F.2d 705 (8th Cir. 1989), cert. denied, 110 S. Ct. 723 (1990)." *Suffolk University Law Review* 24: 1152–58.

Wade, Scott William. 1992. "*People v. Collins*: Participant Monitoring Freed from Warrants." *Detroit College of Law Review* 1992: 909–32.

Warren, Jim, Jay Thorwaldson, and Bruce Koball, eds. 1991. *Computers, Freedom, and Privacy: Proceedings of the First Conference on Computers, Freedom, and Privacy.* Los Alamitos, CA: IEEE Computer Society Press.

Watt, David. 1979. *Law of Electronic Surveillance in Canada.* Toronto: Carswell.

———. 1983. *The Law of Electronic Surveillance in Canada [First Supplement].* Toronto: Carswell.

Weingarten, Fred W. 1988. "Communications Technology: New Challenges to Privacy." *The John Marshall Law Review* 21: 735-53.

Wilkes, Diana. 1991. "The Wiretap Statute: A Haven for Hackers." *Jurimetrics* 4 [Summer]: 415–27.

Witt, Lois R. 1992. "Terminally Nosy: Are Employers Free to Access Our Electronic Mail?" *Dickinson Law Review* 96: 545–71.

Zuckerman, Laurence. 1988. "Sticky Issues in Gumshoe Journalism." *Time* 132 [8 Aug]: 72.

UNITED STATES COURT CASES

Alderman v. U.S., 394 U.S. 165, 22 L. Ed. 2d 176 (1969), reh'g denied, 394 U.S. 939, 22 L. Ed. 2d 475, (1969), on remand sub nom. *U.S. v. Butenko*, 318 F. Supp. 66 (D.N.J. 1970), aff'd, *U.S. v. Butenko*, 494 F.2d 593 (3d Cir. N.J. 1974), cert. denied sub nom. *Ivanov v. United States*, 419 U.S. 881, 42 L. Ed. 2d 121, (1974), cert. denied sub nom. *Barrett v. Zweibon*, 425 U.S.

944, 48 L. Ed. 2d 187, (1976), *appeal after remand, In re Zweibon*, 184 U.S. App. D.C. 167, 565 F.2d 742, 24 Fed. R. Serv. 2d (Callaghan) 448 (1977).

Andes v. Knox, 905 F.2d 188, 1990 U.S. App. LEXIS 8759 (8th Cir. Mo. 1990), *reh'g denied, en banc*, 1990 U.S. App. LEXIS 11844 (8th Cir. 1990), *cert. denied*, 498 U.S. 952, 112 L. Ed. 2d 335, 1990 U.S. LEXIS 5467 (1990).

Angel v. Williams, 12 F.3d 786, 1993 U.S. App. LEXIS 33517, 27 Fed. R. Serv. 3d (Callaghan) 1402 (8th Cir. Mo. 1993).

Anonymous v. Anonymous, 558 F.2d 677 (2d Cir. N.Y. 1977).

Anthony v. U.S., 667 F.2d 870 (10th Cir. Okla. 1981), *cert. denied*, 457 U.S. 1133, 73 L. Ed. 2d 1350 (1982).

Arnold v. State, 803 P.2d 1145, 1990 Okla. Crim. App. LEXIS 79 (Okla. Crim. App. 1990).

Baker v. Cestari, 569 F. Supp. 842 (D.N.H. 1983).

Bender v. Board of Fire & Police Commissioners, 183 Ill. App. 3d 562, 131 Ill. Dec. 881, 539 N.E.2d 234, 1989 Ill. App. LEXIS 650 (1st Dist. 1989), *appeal denied*, 136 Ill. Dec. 581, 545 N.E.2d 105 (Ill. 1989).

Benford v. American Broadcasting Co., Inc. et al., 502 F. Supp. 1159, 6 Media L. Rep. (BNA) 2489 (D. Md. 1980), *aff'd without op.*, 661 F.2d 917 (4th Cir. Md. 1981), *cert. denied, Holton v. Benford*, 454 U.S. 1060, 70 L. Ed. 2d 599 (1981).

Berger v. New York, 388 U.S. 41, 18 L. Ed. 2d 1040, (1967), *conformed to People v. Berger*, 20 N.Y.2d 801, 284 N.Y.S.2d 456, 231 N.E.2d 132 (1967).

Blackmon v. State, 449 So. 2d 1264 (Ala. Ct. App. 1984).

Boddie v. American Broadcasting Co. (1), 731 F.2d 333, 10 Media L. Rep. (BNA) 1923, 15 Fed. R. Evid. Serv. (Callaghan) 833 (6th Cir. Ohio 1984), *on remand, Boddie v. American Broadcasting Co. (2)*, 694 F. Supp. 1304, 1988 U.S. Dist. LEXIS 13787, 16 Media L. Rep. (BNA) 1100 (N.D. Ohio 1988), *aff'd*, 881 F.2d 267, 1989 U.S. App. LEXIS 10968, 16 Media L. Rep. (BNA) 2038 (6th Cir. Ohio 1989), *reh'g denied, en banc*, 1989 U.S. App. LEXIS 18956 (6th Cir. 1989), *cert. denied*, 493 U.S. 1028, 107 L. Ed. 2d 755, 1990 U.S. LEXIS 299 (1990).

Boddie v. American Broadcasting Co. (2), 881 F.2d 267, 1989 U.S. App. LEXIS 10968, 16 Media L. Rep. (BNA) 2038 (6th Cir. Ohio 1989), *reh'g denied, en banc*, 1989 U.S. App. LEXIS 18956 (6th Cir. 14, 1989), *cert. denied*, 493 U.S. 1028, 107 L. Ed. 2d 755, 1990 U.S. LEXIS 299 (1990).

Brown v. American Broadcasting Co., 704 F.2d 1296 (4th Cir. Va. 1983).

Bunnell v. Superior Court, 21 Cal. App. 4th 1811, 26 Cal. Rptr. 2d 819, 1994 Cal. App. LEXIS 64, 94 C.D.O.S. 714, 94 Daily Journal D.A.R. 1105 (3d Dist. 1994).

By-Prod Corp. v. Armen-Berry Co., 668 F.2d 956, 1982-1 Trade Cas. (CCH) P 64514, 33 Fed. R. Serv. 2d (Callaghan) 943, 67 A.L.R. Fed. 419 (7th Cir. Ill. 1982).

California v. Ciraolo, 476 U.S. 207, 90 L. Ed. 2d 210, 4471 (1986), *reh'g denied*, 478 U.S. 1014, 92 L. Ed. 2d 728 (1986).

Chappell v. Redding, 67 N.C. App. 397, 313 S.E.2d 239 (1984), *review denied*, 311 N.C. 399, 319 S.E.2d 268 (1984).
Citron v. Citron, 539 F. Supp. 621 (S.D.N.Y. 1982), *aff'd*, 722 F.2d 14 (2d Cir. N.Y. 1983), *cert. denied*, 466 U.S. 973, 80 L. Ed. 2d 823 (1984).
Cogdill v. Commonwealth, 219 Va. 272, 247 S.E.2d 392, 12 A.L.R.4th 406 (1978).
Commonwealth v. Bloom, 18 Mass. App. Ct. 951, 468 N.E.2d 667 (1984), *review denied*, 393 Mass. 1104, 471 N.E.2d 1354 (1984).
Commonwealth v. Brachbill, 363 Pa. Super. 615, 527 A.2d 113 (1987) *appeal granted*, 516 Pa. 631, 533 A.2d 90 (1987), *later proceeding sub nom. County of Centre v. Musser*, 519 Pa. 380, 548 A.2d 1194, 1988 Pa. LEXIS 246 (1988), *later proceeding, Commonwealth v. Brachbill*, 520 Pa. 533, 555 A.2d 82, 1989 Pa. LEXIS 56 (1989).
Commonwealth v. De Marco, 396 Pa. Super. 357, 578 A.2d 942, 1990 Pa. Super. LEXIS 1764 (1990).
Commonwealth v. Hammond, 308 Pa. Super. 139, 454 A.2d 60 (1982).
Commonwealth v. Henlen, 522 Pa. 514, 564 A.2d 905, 1989 Pa. LEXIS 351 (1989).
Commonwealth v. Kean, 382 Pa. Super. 587, 556 A.2d 374, 1989 Pa. Super. LEXIS 826 (1989), *appeal denied*, 525 Pa. 596, 575 A.2d 563 (1990), *appeal denied*, 525 Pa. 596, 575 A.2d 563 (1990).
Commonwealth v. Penta, 32 Mass. App. Ct. 36, 586 N.E.2d 936, 1992 Mass. App. LEXIS 89 (1992), *review denied*, 412 Mass. 1103, 590 N.E.2d 195, 1992 Mass. LEXIS 206 (1992).
Commonwealth v. Rozanski, 289 Pa. Super. 531, 433 A.2d 1382 (1981).
Commonwealth v. Schaeffer, 1993 Pa. LEXIS 162 (Pa. 1993), *reh'g granted*, 1993 Pa. LEXIS 164 (Pa. 1993).
Commonwealth v. Vitello, 367 Mass. 224, 327 N.E.2d 819 (1975).
Cox v. State, 160 Ga. App. 199, 286 S.E.2d 482 (1981).
Cubic Corp. v. Cheney, 286 U.S. App. D.C. 243, 914 F.2d 1501, 1990 U.S. App. LEXIS 16571 (1990).
Deal v. Spears, 780 F. Supp. 618, 1991 U.S. Dist. LEXIS 18104, 7 I.E.R. Cas. (BNA) 191 (W.D. Ark. 1991), *aff'd*, 980 F.2d 1153, 1992 U.S. App. LEXIS 31203, 8 I.E.R. Cas. (BNA) 105 (8th Cir. Ark. 1992).
Dow Chemical Co. v. U.S., 476 U.S. 227, 90 L. Ed. 2d 226, 24 Env't. Rep. Cas. (BNA) 1385, 16 Envtl. L. Rep. 20679 (1986).
Dunn v. Blue Ridge Telephone Co., 868 F.2d 1578, 1989 U.S. App. LEXIS 4588 (11th Cir. Ga. 1989), *vacated, reh'g granted, en banc*, 888 F.2d 731, 1989 U.S. App. LEXIS 16906 (11th Cir. Ga. 1989).
Epps v. St. Mary's Hospital, Inc., 802 F.2d 412 (11th Cir. Ga. 1986), *reh'g denied, en banc*, 807 F.2d 999 (11th Cir. Ga. 1986).
Florida v. Riley, 488 U.S. 445, 102 L. Ed. 2d 835, 1989 U.S. LEXIS 580 (1989), *reh'g denied*, 490 U.S. 1014, 104 L. Ed. 2d 172, 1989 U.S. LEXIS 1779 (1989).
Fordyce v. City of Seattle, 840 F. Supp. 784, 1993 U.S. Dist. LEXIS 12301, 21 Media L. Rep. (BNA) 2177 (W.D. Wash. 1993).

Frio v. Superior Court, 203 Cal. App. 3d 1480, 250 Cal. Rptr. 819, 1988 Cal. App. LEXIS 788 (2d Dist. 1988).

Galella v. Onassis, 353 F. Supp. 196 (S.D.N.Y. 1972), *aff'd in part and rev'd in part*, 487 F.2d 986, 1 Media L. Rep. (BNA) 2425, 17 Fed. R. Serv. 2d (Callaghan) 1205, 28 A.L.R. Fed. 879 (2d Cir. N.Y. 1973).

Grandbouche v. Adams, 529 F. Supp. 545 (D. Colo. 1982), *later proceeding sub nom.*

Grandbouche v. Clancy, 825 F.2d 1463, 8 Fed. R. Serv. 3d (Callaghan) 1037 (10th Cir. Colo. 1987), *appeal after remand sub nom. Grandbouche v. Lovell*, 913 F.2d 835, 1990 U.S. App. LEXIS 15575, 17 Fed. R. Serv. 3d (Callaghan) 1042 (10th Cir. Colo. 1990).

Greenfield v. Kootenai County, 752 F.2d 1387 (9th Cir. Idaho 1985).

Griggs-Ryan v. Smith, 904 F.2d 112, 1990 U.S. App. LEXIS 9239 (1st Cir. Me. 1990).

Harry R. v. Esther R., 134 Misc. 2d 404, 510 N.Y.S.2d 792 (1986).

Hester v. U.S., 265 U.S. 57, 68 L. Ed. 898 (1924).

Hirschey v. Menlow, 89 Or. App. 108, 747 P.2d 402 (1987).

In re John Doe Trader Number One, 894 F.2d 240, 1990 U.S. App. LEXIS 994 (7th Cir. Ill. 1990).

In re King World Prods., Inc., 898 F.2d 56, 1990 U.S. App. LEXIS 3363 (6th Cir. Mich. 1990).

In re Marriage of Lopp, 268 Ind. 690, 378 N.E.2d 414 (1978), *cert. denied*, 439 U.S. 1116, 59 L. Ed. 2d 76 (1979).

Jacks v. State, 271 Ind. 611, 394 N.E.2d 166 (1979), *habeas corpus proceeding sub nom. Jacks v. Duckworth*, 486 F. Supp. 1366 (N.D. Ind. 1980), *aff'd*, 651 F.2d 480 (7th Cir. Ind. 1981), *cert. denied*, 454 U.S. 1147, 71 L. Ed. 2d 300 (1982), *reh'g denied*, 456 U.S. 984, 72 L. Ed. 2d 865 (1982), *habeas corpus proceeding*, 857 F.2d 394, 1988 U.S. App. LEXIS 12881 (7th Cir. Ind. 1988), *cert. denied*, 489 U.S. 1017, 103 L. Ed. 2d 195, 1989 U.S. LEXIS 1032 (1989).

James v. U.S., 135 U.S. App. D.C. 314, 418 F.2d 1150 (1969).

Jessee v. State, 640 P.2d 56 (Wyo. 1982), *reh'g denied*, 643 P.2d 681 (Wyo. 1982).

Jewelcor, Inc. v. Pre-Fab Panelwall, Inc., 397 Pa. Super. 78, 579 A.2d 940, 1990 Pa. Super. LEXIS 2552 (1990).

Kassap v. Seitz, 315 Md. 155, 553 A.2d 714, 1989 Md. LEXIS 28 (1989).

Katz v. U.S., 389 U.S. 347, 19 L. Ed. 2d 576 (1967).

Kirk v. State, 526 So. 2d 223, 1988 La. LEXIS 1285 (La. 1988).

Kotrla v. Kotrla, 718 S.W.2d 853 (Tex. App. Corpus Christi 1986), *writ ref'd n.r.e.* (Jan. 21, 1987).

La Porte v. State, 512 So. 2d 984, 12 Fla. L. Weekly 2007 (Fla. Dist. Ct. App. 2d Dist. 1987), *review denied*, 519 So. 2d 987, 1988 Fla. LEXIS 54 (Fla. 1988).

Lopp v. Lopp, 439 U.S. 1116, 59 L. Ed. 2d 76 (1979).

Malouche v. JH Mgmt. Co., 839 F.2d 1024, 1988 U.S. App. LEXIS 2109 (4th Cir. S.C. 1988).
McCray v. State, 84 Md. App. 513, 581 A.2d 45, 1990 Md. App. LEXIS 160 (1990), *cert. denied*, 322 Md. 131, 586 A.2d 14 (1991).
Meredith v. Gavin, 446 F.2d 794 (8th Cir. Mo. 1971).
Mimms v. Mimms, 780 S.W.2d 739, 1989 Tenn. App. LEXIS 556 (Tenn. Ct. App. 1989).
Montone v. Radio Shack, a Div. of Tandy Corp., 698 F. Supp. 92, 1988 U.S. Dist. LEXIS 14610, 26 Fed. R. Evid. Serv. (Callaghan) 1522 (E.D. Pa. 1988).
Nader v. General Motors Corp., 25 N.Y.2d 560, 307 N.Y.S.2d 647, 255 N.E.2d 765 (1970).
Nardone v. U.S., 302 U.S. 379, 82 L. Ed. 314 (1937).
Nardone v. U.S., 308 U.S. 338, 84 L. Ed. 307 (1939).
Oliver v. U.S., 466 U.S. 170, 80 L. Ed. 2d 214 (1984), *on remand sub nom. State v. Thornton*, 485 A.2d 952 (Me. 1984).
Olmstead v. U.S., 277 U.S. 438, 72 L. Ed. 944, 66 A.L.R. 376 (1928).
People v. Castania, 73 Misc. 2d 166, 340 N.Y.S.2d 829 (1973).
People v. Collins, 438 Mich. 8, 475 N.W.2d 684, 1991 Mich. LEXIS 2118 (1991).
People v. Dezek, 107 Mich. App. 78, 308 N.W.2d 652 (1981).
People v. Fata, 139 Misc. 2d 979, 529 N.Y.S.2d 683, 1988 N.Y. Misc. LEXIS 273 (1988), *later proceeding*, 159 A.D.2d 180, 559 N.Y.S.2d 348, 1990 N.Y. App. Div. LEXIS 8774 (2d Dep't 1990), *appeal denied*, 76 N.Y.2d 985, 563 N.Y.S.2d 774, 565 N.E.2d 523, 1990 N.Y. LEXIS 4585 (1990).
People v. Gervasi, 90 Ill. App. 3d 1117, 46 Ill. Dec. 369, 414 N.E.2d 91 (1st Dist. 1980), *aff'd in part and rev'd in part*, 89 Ill. 2d 522, 61 Ill. Dec. 515, 434 N.E.2d 1112 (1982).
People v. Henderson, 220 Cal. App. 3d 1632, 270 Cal. Rptr. 248, 1990 Cal. App. LEXIS 589 (4th Dist. 1990).
People v. Hicks, 49 Ill. App. 3d 421, 7 Ill. Dec. 279, 364 N.E.2d 440 (1st Dist. 1977).
People v. Jones, 30 Cal. App. 3d 852, 106 Cal. Rptr. 749 (4th Dist. 1973), *appeal dismissed, California v. Jones*, 414 U.S. 804, 38 L. Ed 2d 40 (1973).
People v. Klingenberg, 34 Ill. App. 3d 705, 339 N.E.2d 456 (2d Dist. 1975).
People v. Nicoletti, 84 Misc. 2d 385, 375 N.Y.S.2d 720 (1975).
People v. Otto, 2 Cal. 4th 1088, 9 Cal. Rptr. 2d 596, 831 P.2d 1178, 1992 Cal. LEXIS 3050, 92 C.D.O.S. 6107, 92 Daily Journal D.A.R 9617 (1992), *reh'g denied*, 1992 Cal. LEXIS 4223 (Cal. Aug. 20, 1992), *later proceeding*, 1992 Cal. LEXIS 5155 (Cal. Oct. 16, 1992), *cert. denied sub nom. California v. Otto*, 121 L. Ed. 2d 338, 1992 U.S. LEXIS 6859, 113 S. Ct. 414 (U.S. 1992).
People v. Patrick, 46 Mich. App. 678, 208 N.W.2d 604 (1973).
People v. Pedersen, 86 Cal. App. 3d 987, 150 Cal. Rptr. 577 (4th Dist. 1978).

People v. Regains, 187 Ill. App. 3d 713, 135 Ill. Dec. 522, 543 N.E.2d 1090, 1989 Ill. App. LEXIS 1336 (3d Dist. 1989), *appeal denied*, 139 Ill. Dec. 520, 548 N.E.2d 1076 (Ill. 1990).

People v. Schnurr, 206 Ill. App. 3d 522, 151 Ill. Dec. 674, 564 N.E.2d 1336, 1990 Ill. App. LEXIS 1891 (2d Dist. 1990), *appeal denied*, 137 Ill. 2d 670, 156 Ill. Dec. 567, 571 N.E.2d 154 (1991).

People v. Shinkle, 128 Ill. 2d 480, 132 Ill. Dec. 432, 539 N.E.2d 1238, 1989 Ill. LEXIS 82 (1989).

People v. Siripongs, 45 Cal. 3d 548, 247 Cal. Rptr. 729, 754 P.2d 1306, 1988 Cal. LEXIS 113 (1988), *cert. denied sub nom. Siripongs v. California*, 488 U.S. 1019, 102 L. Ed. 2d 810, 1989 U.S. LEXIS 101 (1989), *stay granted sub nom. In re Siripongs*, 1989 Cal. LEXIS 1143 (Cal. Mar. 15, 1989), *vacated*, 1989 Cal. LEXIS 4105 (Cal. Aug. 16, 1989), *habeas corpus proceeding, remanded sub nom. Siripongs v. Calderon*, 35 F.3d 1308, 1994 U.S. App. LEXIS 16384, 94 C.D.O.S. 5105, 94 Daily Journal D.A.R. 9410 (9th Cir. Cal. 1994), *amended, reh'g, en banc, denied*, 1994 U.S. App. LEXIS 28305, 94 C.D.O.S. 7830, 94 Daily Journal D.A.R. 14461 (9th Cir. Cal. 1994), *cert. denied*, 130 L. Ed. 2d 1127, 1995 U.S. LEXIS 1527, 63 U.S.L.W. 3628 (U.S. 1995).

People v. Teicher, 52 N.Y.2d 638, 439 N.Y.S.2d 846, 422 N.E.2d 506 (1981).

People v. Wehde, 210 Ill. App. 3d 56, 154 Ill. Dec. 689, 568 N.E.2d 910, 1991 Ill. App. LEXIS 293 (2d Dist. 1991).

People v. White, 209 Ill. App. 3d 844, 153 Ill. Dec. 910, 567 N.E.2d 1368, 1991 Ill. App. LEXIS 283 (5th Dist. 1991), *appeal denied*, 139 Ill. 2d 604, 159 Ill. Dec. 115, 575 N.E.2d 922 (1991).

People v. Wilson, 17 Cal. App. 3d 598, 94 Cal. Rptr. 923 (4th Dist. 1971).

People v. Winograd, 68 N.Y.2d 383, 509 N.Y.S.2d 512, 502 N.E.2d 189 (1986).

Pine v. Rust, 404 Mass. 411, 535 N.E.2d 1247, 1989 Mass. LEXIS 86 (1989).

Reed v. Dick, 200 Cal. App. 3d 469, 246 Cal. Rptr. 131, 1988 Cal. App. LEXIS 337 (1st Dist. 1988), *op. withdrawn by order of ct.*, 38 CAL 3D 355.

Ribas v. Clark, 38 Cal. 3d 355, 212 Cal. Rptr. 143, 696 P.2d 637, 49 A.L.R.4th 417 (1985).

Ricks v. State, 312 Md. 11, 537 A.2d 612, 1988 Md. LEXIS 50 (1988), *cert. denied, Ricks v. Maryland*, 488 U.S. 832, 102 L. Ed. 2d 66, 1988 U.S. LEXIS 3635 (1988).

Rodgers v. Wood, 910 F.2d 444, 1990 U.S. App. LEXIS 14199, 17 Fed. R. Serv. 3d (Callaghan) 885 (7th Cir. Wis. 1990), *reh'g denied, en banc*, 1990 U.S. App. LEXIS 16140 (7th Cir. Wis. 1990).

Royal Health Care Servs., Inc. v. Jefferson-Pilot Life Ins. Co., 924 F.2d 215, 1991 U.S. App. LEXIS 2713 (11th Cir. Fla. 1991).

Scheib v. Grant, 814 F. Supp. 736, 1993 U.S. Dist. LEXIS 1612 (N.D. Ill. 1993), *cert. denied*, 130 L. Ed. 2d 280, 1994 U.S. LEXIS 7119 (U.S. 1994).

Scutieri v. Estate of Revitz, 683 F. Supp. 795, 1988 U.S. Dist. LEXIS 7944 (S.D. Fla. 1988), *mot. denied*, 1993 U.S. Dist. LEXIS 10478, 7 Fla. L. Weekly Fed. D 340 (S.D. Fla. 1993).
Silverman v. U.S., 365 U.S. 505, 5 L. Ed. 2d 734, 97 A.L.R.2d 1277 (1961).
Smayda v. U.S., 352 F.2d 251 (9th Cir. Cal. 1965), *cert. denied*, 382 U.S. 981, 15 L. Ed. 2d 471 (1966).
Smith v. Associated Bureaus, Inc., 177 Ill. App. 3d 286, 126 Ill. Dec. 616, 532 N.E.2d 301, 1988 Ill. App. LEXIS 1885 (1st Dist. 1988), *appeal denied*, 126 Ill. 2d 566, 133 Ill. Dec. 677, 541 N.E.2d 1115 (1989).
Smith v. State, 283 Md. 156, 389 A.2d 858 (1978), *aff'd, Smith v. Maryland*, 442 U.S. 735, 61 L. Ed. 2d 220, 99 S. Ct. 2577 (1979).
Standiford v. Standiford, 89 Md. App. 326, 598 A.2d 495, 1991 Md. App. LEXIS 225 (1991), *cert. denied*, 325 Md. 526, 601 A.2d 1101 (1992).
State v. Bichsel, 101 Or. App. 257, 790 P.2d 1142, 1990 Ore. App. LEXIS 450 (1990).
State v. Brooks, 157 Vt. 490, 601 A.2d 963, 1991 Vt. LEXIS 219 (1991).
State v. Delaurier, 488 A.2d 688 (R.I. 1985).
State v. Dillon, 191 W. Va. 648, 447 S.E.2d 583, 1994 W. Va. LEXIS 148 (1994).
State v. Dimeo, 304 Or. 469, 747 P.2d 353 (1987).
State v. Ford, 108 Ariz. 404, 499 P.2d 699 (1972), *cert. denied, Ford v. Arizona*, 409 U.S. 1128, 35 L. Ed. 2d 261, 93 S. Ct. 950 (1973).
State v. Gibson, 255 Kan. 474, 874 P.2d 1122, 1994 Kan. LEXIS 85 (1994).
State v. Gonzalez, 71 Wash. App. 715, 862 P.2d 598, 1993 Wash. App. LEXIS 422 (1993), *review denied*, 123 Wash. 2d 1022, 875 P.2d 635, 1994 Wash. LEXIS 257 (1994).
State v. Grullon, 212 Conn. 195, 562 A.2d 481, 1989 Conn. LEXIS 214 (1989).
State v. Hamblin, 505 N.W.2d 140, 1993 Wis. LEXIS 683 (Wis. 1993).
State v. Howard, 62 Ohio App. 3d 910, 577 N.E.2d 749, 1990 Ohio App. LEXIS 4357 (Clark County 1990), *dismissed, mot. overruled, State v. Howard*, 58 Ohio St. 3d 713, 570 N.E.2d 277, 1991 Ohio LEXIS 729 (1991).
State v. Howard, 235 Kan. 236, 679 P.2d 197 (1984).
State v. Jones, 562 So. 2d 740, 1990 Fla. App. LEXIS 3115, 15 Fla. L. Weekly D 1279 (Fla. Dist. Ct. App. 3d Dist. 1990).
State v. Knobel, 97 Or. App. 559, 777 P.2d 985, 1989 Ore. App. LEXIS 867, 16 Media L. Rep. (BNA) 2478 (1989), *review denied*, 309 Or. 522, 789 P.2d 1387, 1990 Ore. LEXIS 244 (1990).
State v. Limberhand, 117 Idaho 456, 788 P.2d 857, 1990 Ida. App. LEXIS 52 (Ct. App. 1990).
State v. McVeigh, 224 Conn. 593, 620 A.2d 133, 1993 Conn. LEXIS 23 (1993).

State v. Raymer, 61 Wash. App. 516, 810 P.2d 1383, 1991 Wash. App. LEXIS 185 (1991), *review denied*, 117 Wash. 2d 1022, 818 P.2d 1098, 1991 Wash. LEXIS 382 (1991).

State v. Reyes, 107 Nev. 191, 808 P.2d 544, 1991 Nev. LEXIS 30 (1991).

State v. Shaw, 103 N.C. App. 268, 404 S.E.2d 887, 1991 N.C. App. LEXIS 646 (1991), *writ denied, stay denied*, 407 S.E.2d 528, 1991 N.C. LEXIS 507 (N.C. 1991), *review denied*, 329 N.C. 503, 407 S.E.2d 548, 1991 N.C. LEXIS 541 (1991).

State v. Slemmer, 48 Wash. App. 48, 738 P.2d 281 (1987).

State v. Smith, 149 Wis. 2d 89, 438 N.W.2d 571, 1989 Wis. LEXIS 42 (1989).

State v. Stachler, 58 Haw. 412, 570 P.2d 1323 (1977).

State v. Stockfleth, 311 Or. 40, 804 P.2d 471, 1991 Ore. LEXIS 8 (1991).

State v. Tucker, 626 So. 2d 707, 1993 La. LEXIS 1803 (La. 1993), *adopted, reaff'd, on reh'g*, 626 So. 2d 720, 1993 La. LEXIS 2925 (La. 1993).

State v. West, 553 So. 2d 945, 1989 La. App. LEXIS 2181 (La. Ct. App. 4th Cir. 1989), *cert. denied*, 558 So. 2d 567, 1990 La. LEXIS 578 (La. 1990), *appeal after remand*, 578 So. 2d 1016, 1991 La. App. LEXIS 753 (La. Ct. App. 4th Cir. 1991).

Stockler v. Garratt, 893 F.2d 856, 1990 U.S. App. LEXIS 281 (6th Cir. Mich. 1990), *reh'g denied, en banc*, Stockler v. Garratt, 1990 U.S. App. LEXIS 4845 (6th Cir. Feb. 27, 1990), *appeal after remand*, 974 F.2d 730, 1992 U.S. App. LEXIS 20963 (6th Cir. Mich. 1992), *reh'g, en banc, denied*, 1992 U.S. App. LEXIS 28951 (6th Cir. Oct. 23, 1992).

Stowe v. Devoy, 588 F.2d 336 (2d Cir. N.Y. 1978), *cert. denied*, 442 U.S. 931, 61 L. Ed. 2d 299 (1979).

Tarnoff v. Wellington Financial Corp., 696 F. Supp. 151, 1988 U.S. Dist. LEXIS 11445 (E.D. Pa. 1988).

Texas v. Brown, 460 U.S. 730, 75 L. Ed. 2d 502 (1983), *on remand Brown v. State*, 657 S.W.2d 797 (Tex. Crim. App. 1983).

Thompson v. Predaina, No. 88-93C (S.D. Ind., *dismissed* Aug. 10, 1988).

Tyler v. Berodt, 877 F.2d 705, 1989 U.S. App. LEXIS 8570 (8th Cir. Iowa 1989), *cert. denied*, 493 U.S. 1022, 107 L. Ed. 2d 743, 1990 U.S. LEXIS 224 (1990).

U.S. v. Aguilar, 883 F.2d 662 (9th Cir. Ariz. 1989), *cert. denied, Socorro Pardo v. U.S.*, 498 U.S. 1046, 112 L. Ed. 2d 771, 1991 U.S. LEXIS 350 3481 (1991).

U.S. v. Arredondo-Hernandez, 574 F.2d 1312 (5th Cir. Tex. 1978).

U.S. v. Arriaga, 1993 U.S. Dist. LEXIS 18033 (D.P.R. Oct. 18, 1993).

U.S. v. Bast, 161 U.S. App. D.C. 312, 495 F.2d 138 (1974).

U.S. v. Bernal, 884 F.2d 1518, 1989 U.S. App. LEXIS 13866, 28 Fed. R. Evid. Serv. (Callaghan) 894 (1st Cir. P.R. 1989).

U.S. v. Biasucci, 786 F.2d 504 (2d Cir. N.Y. 1986), *cert. denied, Biasucci v. U.S.*, 479 U.S. 827, 93 L. Ed. 2d 54 3232 (1986), *cert. denied, Capo v. U.S.*, 479 U.S. 827, 93 L. Ed. 2d 56 (1986).

U.S. v. Burroughs, 564 F.2d 1111 (4th Cir. S.C. 1977).
U.S. v. Bynum, 360 F. Supp. 400 (S.D.N.Y. 1973), *aff'd*, 485 F.2d 490 (2d Cir. N.Y. 1973), *vacated, Bynum v. U.S.*, 417 U.S. 903, 41 L. Ed. 2d 209 (1974), *conformed to, U.S. v. Bynum*, 386 F. Supp. 449 (S.D.N.Y. 1974), *aff'd, U.S. v. Bynum*, 513 F.2d 533 (2d Cir. 1975), *cert. denied, Bynum v. U.S.*, 423 U.S. 952, 46 L. Ed. 2d 277 (1975).
U.S. v. Carroll, 337 F. Supp. 1260 (D.D.C. 1971).
U.S. v. Christman, 375 F. Supp. 1354 (N.D. Cal. 1974).
U.S. v. Coven, 662 F.2d 162, 9 Fed. R. Evid. Serv. (Callaghan) 475 (2d Cir. N.Y. 1981), *cert. denied, Coven v. U.S.*, 456 U.S. 916, 72 L. Ed. 2d 176 (1982).
U.S. v. Cuevas-Sanchez, 821 F.2d 248 (5th Cir. Tex. 1987).
U.S. v. Donovan, 429 U.S. 413, 50 L. Ed. 2d 652 (1977), *conformed to*, 552 F.2d 735 (6th Cir. Ohio 1977).
U.S. v. Dorfman, 690 F.2d 1217 (7th Cir. Ill. 1932).
U.S. v. Duncan, 598 F.2d 839, 4 Fed. R. Evid. Serv. (Callaghan) 848 (4th Cir. N.C. 1979), *cert. denied, Duncan v. United States*, 444 U.S. 871, 62 L. Ed. 2d 96 (1979).
U.S. v. Dunn, 480 U.S. 294, 94 L. Ed. 2d 326 4251 (1987), *reh'g denied, U.S. v. Dunn*, 481 U.S. 1024, 95 L. Ed. 2d 519 (1987), *on remand*, 817 F.2d 18 (5th Cir. Tex. 1987).
U.S. v. Fisch, 474 F.2d 1071 (9th Cir. Cal. 1973), *cert. denied*, 412 U.S. 921, 37 L. Ed. 2d 148, (1973).
U.S. v. Giordano, 416 U.S. 505, 40 L. Ed. 2d 341 (1974).
U.S. v. Gomez, 900 F.2d 43, 1990 U.S. App. LEXIS 6063 (5th Cir. Tex. 1990), *amended, reh'g denied*, 1990 U.S. App. LEXIS 9674 (5th Cir. June 12, 1990), *appeal after remand*, 947 F.2d 737, 1991 U.S. App. LEXIS 26490 (5th Cir. Tex. 1991), *cert. denied*, 117 L. Ed. 2d 642, 1992 U.S. LEXIS 1882 3653 (U.S. 1992).
U.S. v. Hall, 488 F.2d 193 (9th Cir. Ariz. 1973).
U.S. v. Harpel, 493 F.2d 346 (10th Cir. Colo. 1974).
U.S. v. Havens, 446 U.S. 620, 64 L. Ed. 2d 559, 6 Fed. R. Evid. Serv. (Callaghan) 1 (1980), *reh'g denied*, 448 U.S. 911, 65 L. Ed. 2d 1172 (1980), *on remand*, 625 F.2d 1311 (5th Cir. Fla. 1980), *cert. denied*, 450 U.S. 995, 68 L. Ed. 2d 195 (1981).
U.S. v. Horton, 601 F.2d 319 (7th Cir. Ill. 1979), *cert. denied*, 444 U.S. 937, 62 L. Ed. 2d 197, (1979).
U.S. v. Jackson, 588 F.2d 1046, 4 Fed. R. Evid. Serv. (Callaghan) 245, 49 A.L.R. Fed. 461 (5th Cir. Ala. 1979), *reh'g denied*, 591 F.2d 1343 (5th Cir. Ala. 1979), *cert. denied*, 442 U.S. 941, 61 L. Ed. 2d 310 (1979).
U.S. v. Karo, 468 U.S. 705, 82 L. Ed. 2d 530 (1984), *reh'g denied, U.S. v. Karo*, 468 U.S. 1250, 82 L. Ed. 2d 942 (1984).
U.S. v. King, 335 F. Supp. 523 (S.D. Cal. 1971), *aff'd in part and rev'd in part*, 478 F.2d 494 (9th Cir. Cal. 1973), *cert. denied sub nom. Light v. U.S.*, 414

U.S. 846, 38 L. Ed. 2d 94 (1973), *cert. denied sub nom. U.S. v. King*, 417 U.S. 920, 41 L. Ed. 2d 226 (1974).

U.S. v. Knotts, 460 U.S. 276, 75 L. Ed. 2d 55 (1983).

U.S. v. Koyomejian, 946 F.2d 1450, 1992 U.S. App. LEXIS 803 (9th Cir. Cal. 1991).

U.S. v. Laetividal-Gonzalez, 939 F.2d 1455, 1991 U.S. App. LEXIS 19772 (11th Cir. Fla. 1991), *cert. denied sub nom. Ocampo v. U.S.*, 117 L. Ed. 2d 505, 1992 U.S. LEXIS 1418 (U.S. 1992).

U.S. v. Leta, 332 F. Supp. 1357 (M.D. Pa. 1971).

U.S. v. McIntyre, 582 F.2d 1221 (9th Cir. Ariz. 1978).

U.S. v. McKinnon, 985 F.2d 525, 1993 U.S. App. LEXIS 4226, 7 Fla. L. Weekly Fed. C 90 (11th Cir. Fla. 1993), *cert. denied*, 126 L. Ed. 2d 94, 1993 U.S. LEXIS 5356 (U.S. 1993).

U.S. v. Mesa-Rincon, 911 F.2d 1433, 1990 U.S. App. LEXIS 14187 (10th Cir. Kan. 1990).

U.S. v. Miller, 720 F.2d 227 (1st Cir. Mass. 1983), *cert. denied*, 464 U.S. 1073, 79 L. Ed. 2d 220 (1984).

U.S. v. Mitro, 880 F.2d 1480, 1989 U.S. App. LEXIS 10979 (1st Cir. Mass. 1989).

U.S. v. Mora, 821 F.2d 860 (1st Cir. Mass. 1987).

U.S. v. Napier, 451 F.2d 552 (5th Cir. Fla. 1971).

U.S. v. Nelson, 837 F.2d 1519, 1988 U.S. App. LEXIS 2292 (11th Cir. Fla. 1988), *reh'g denied, en banc*, 845 F.2d 1032, 1988 U.S. App. LEXIS 13045 (11th Cir. Fla. 1988), *cert. denied sub nom. Waldhart v. U.S.*, 488 U.S. 829, 102 L. Ed. 2d 58, 1988 U.S. LEXIS 3787 (1988).

U.S. v. Pageau, 526 F. Supp. 1221 (N.D.N.Y. 1981).

U.S. v. Peterson, 812 F.2d 486 (9th Cir. Cal. 1987).

U.S. v. Regan, 706 F. Supp. 1102, 1989 U.S. Dist. LEXIS 959 (S.D.N.Y. 1989), *later proceeding*, 713 F. Supp. 629, 1989 U.S. Dist. LEXIS 4870, Fed. Sec. L. Rep. (CCH) P 94481 (S.D.N.Y. 1989), *later proceeding*, 726 F. Supp. 447, 1989 U.S. Dist. LEXIS 14620 (S.D.N.Y. 1989), *later proceeding*, 937 F.2d 823, 1991 U.S. App. LEXIS 13555, Fed. Sec. L. Rep. (CCH) P 96062, 91-2 U.S. Tax Cas. (CCH) P 50351, 68 A.F.T.R.2d (P-H) P 91-5215 (2d Cir. N.Y. 1991), *amended*, 946 F.2d 188, 1991 U.S. App. LEXIS 24444 (2d Cir. N.Y. 1991), *cert. denied sub nom. Zarzecki v. U.S.*, 119 L. Ed. 2d 200, 1992 U.S. LEXIS 3145 (U.S. 1992).

U.S. v. Ross, 713 F.2d 389 (8th Cir. Ark. 1983).

U.S. v. Ruppel, 666 F.2d 261, 9 Fed. R. Evid. Serv. (Callaghan) 1170 (5th Cir. Tex. 1982), *reh'g denied*, 671 F.2d 1378 (5th Cir. Tex. 1982), *cert. denied*, 458 U.S. 1107, 73 L. Ed. 2d 1369, *reh'g denied*, 458 U.S. 1132, 73 L. Ed. 2d 1402 (1982), *later proceeding*, 724 F.2d 507 (5th Cir. Tex. 1984), *later proceeding sub nom. United States v. "Monkey"*, 725 F.2d 1007 (5th Cir. Tex. 1984), *reh'g denied*, 729 F.2d 779 (5th Cir. Tex. 1984).

U.S. v. San Martin, 469 F.2d 5 (2d Cir. N.Y. 1972), *cert. denied*, 410 U.S. 934, 35 L. Ed. 2d 598 (1973).
U.S. v. Schweihs, 569 F.2d 965 (5th Cir. Fla. 1978).
U.S. v. Shields, 675 F.2d 1152 (11th Cir. Fla. 1982), *cert. denied*, 459 U.S. 858, 74 L. Ed. 2d 112 (1982), *cert. denied sub nom. Quick v. U.S.*, 459 U.S. 1015, 74 L. Ed. 2d 508, (1982).
U.S. v. Smith, 712 F.2d 702 (1st Cir. Mass. 1983).
U.S. v. Taketa, 923 F.2d 665, 1991 U.S. App. LEXIS 86, 91 C D.O.S. 314, 91 Daily Journal D.A.R. 307 (9th Cir. Nev. 1991).
U.S. v. Tirinkian, 502 F. Supp. 620 (D.N.D. 1980).
U.S. v. Torres, 751 F.2d 875 (7th Cir. Ill. 1984), *on remand*, 602 F. Supp. 1458, 11 Media L. Rep. (BNA) 1661 (N.D Ill. 1985), *cert. denied sub nom. Rodriguez v. U.S.*, 470 U.S. 1087, 85 L. Ed. 2d 150 (1985).
U.S. v. Truglio, 731 F.2d 1123 (4th Cir. W. Va. 1984), *cert. denied*, 469 U.S. 862, 83 L. Ed. 2d 130 (1984).
U.S. v. Turk, 526 F.2d 654 (5th Cir. Fla. 1976), *reh'g denied*, 529 F.2d 523 (5th Cir. Fla. 1976), *cert. denied*, 429 U.S. 823, 50 L. Ed. 2d 84 (1976).
U.S. v. Wright, 146 U.S. App. D.C. 126, 449 F.2d 1355 (1971), *cert. denied*, 405 U.S. 947, 30 L. Ed. 2d 817 (1972).
Walder v. U.S., 347 U.S. 62, 98 L. Ed. 503 (1954).
Walker v. Darby, 911 F.2d 1573, 1990 U.S. App. LEXIS 16510, 5 I.E.R. Cas. (BNA) 1342 (11th Cir. Ala. 1990).
Ward v. State, 787 S.W.2d 116, 1990 Tex. App. LEXIS 439 (Tex. App. Corpus Christi 1990), *pet. for discretionary review ref'd*, (Sept. 12, 1990).
White v. Weiss, 535 F.2d 1067 (8th Cir. Neb. 1976).
Williams v. Poulos, 22 M.L.W. 729, 14 R.I.L.W. 682 (1st Cir. 1993).
Wyoming Dept. of Employment, Div. of Unemployment Ins. v. Patrick, 818 P.2d 54, 1991 Wyo. LEXIS 149 (Wyo. 1991).

Canadian Court Cases

Canadian Civil Liberties Union v. Canada, 91 D.L.R. (4th) 33, 32 A.C.W.S. (3d) 721, 15
W.C.B. (2d) 512, 1992 (O.C. Gen. Div.).
In Re Copeland and Adamson et al., 7 C.C.C. (2d) 393, 1972 (Ont. H.C.).
The King v. County of London Quarter Sessions Appeals Committee, Ex Parte Metropolitan Police Commissioner, 1 K.B. 670 (1947) [1948].
R. v. Aranda, 69 C.C.C. (3d) 420, 15 W.C.B. (2d) 20, 1992 (O.C. Gen. Div.).
R. v. Barnes, 63 C.C.C. (3d) 1, 12 W.C.B. (2d) 272, 1991 (S C.C.).
R. v. Bisson, 94 C.C.C. (3d) 94. 1994 (S.C.C.).
R. v. Blackmore, 67 C.C.C. (3d) 67, 14 W.C.B. (2d) 7, 1991 (N.B.C.A.).

R. v. Clymore, 74 C.C.C. (3d) 217, 16 W.C.B. (2d) 538, 1992 (B.C.S.C.).
R. v. Duarte, 53 C.C.C. (3d) 1, 65 D.L.R. (4th) 240, 9 W.C.B. (2d) 230, 1990 (S.C.C.).
R. v. Dunn, 28 C.C.C. (2d) 538, 33 C.R.N.S. 299, 16 N.S.R. (2d) 527, 1975 (Co. Ct.).
R. v. Elzein, 82 C.C.C. (3d) 455, 1993 (Q.C.A.).
R. v. F. (H.), 55 C.C.C. (3d) 286, 9 W.C.B. (2d) 593, 1990 (A.C.A.).
R. v. Fegan, 80 C.C.C. (3d) 356, 1993 (O.C.A.).
R. v. Garofoli, 60 C.C.C. (3d) 161, 11 W.C.B. (2d) 342, 1990 (S.C.C.).
R. v. Giesecke, 82 C.C.C. (3d) 331, 1993 (O.C.A.).
R. v. Goldman, 51 C.C.C. (2d) 1, 108 D.L.R. (3d) 17, [1980] 1 S.C.R. 976, 13 C.R. (3d) 228, 30 N.R. 453, 1979 (S.C.C.).
R. v. Grant, 84 C.C.C. (3d) 173 1993 (S.C.C.).
R. v. Greffe, 55 C.C.C. (3d) 161, 1990 (S.C.C.).
R. v. Irwin and Sansone et al., 32 C.R.N.S. 398, 1976 (O.C.A.).
R. v. Kokesch, 61 C.C.C. (3d) 207, 11 W.C.B. (2d) 349, 1990 (S.C.C.).
R. v. Mason, 39 D.L.R. 54, 1918 (Que. P.M.C.).
R. v. McQueen, 25 C.C.C. (2d) 262, [1975] 6 W.W.R. 604, 1975 (A.C.A.).
R. v. Miller et al., 12 C.C.C. (3d) 54, 1984 (B.C.C.A.).
R. v. Montoute, 62 C.C.C. (3d) 481, 12 W.C.B. (2d) 107, 1991 (A.C.A.).
R. v. Plant, 84 C.C.C. (3d) 203, 1993 (S.C.C.).
R. v. Rodney, 65 C.C.C. (3d) 304, 13 W.C.B. (2d) 68, 1991 (B.C.S.C.).
R. v. Rosen, 51 C.C.C. (2d) 65, 108 D.L.R. (3d) 60, [1980] 1 S.C.R. 961, 13 C.R. (3d) 214, 30 N.R. 483, 1976 (Ont. H.C.).
R. v. Sandhu, 82 C.C.C. (3d) 236, 1993 (B.C.C.A.).
R. v. Smyk, 86 C.C.C. (3d) 63, 1993 (M.C.A.).
R. v. Solomon, 85 C.C.C. (3d) 496, 1993 (Que. M.C.).
R. v. Spennato, 65 C.C.C. (3d) 97, 13 W.C.B. (2d) 111, 1991 (O.C.A.).
R. v. Tam, 80 C.C.C. (3d) 476, 1993 (B.C.S.C.).
R. v. Thompson, 59 C.C.C. (3d) 225, 73 D.L.R. (4th) 596 11 W.C.B. (2d) 219, 1990 (S.C.C.).
R. v. Unger, 83 C.C.C. (3d) 228, 1993 (M.C.A.).
R. v. Welsh and Ianuzzi (No. 6), 32 C.C.C. (2d) 363, 1977 (O.C.A.).
R. v. Wiggins, 53 C.C.C. (3d) 476, 9 W.C.B. (2d) 200, 1990 (S.C.C.).
R. v. Wijesinha, 88 C.C.C. (3d) 116, 1994 (O.C.A.).
R. v. Wile, 58 C.C.C. (3d) 85, 10 W.C.B. (2d) 428, 1990 (O.C.A.).
R. v. Wills, 70 C.C.C. (3d) 529, 15 W.C.B. (2d) 415, 1992 (O.C.A.).
R. v. Wong, 60 C.C.C. (3d) 460, 11 W.C.B. (2d) 350, 1990 (S.C.C.).

United States Federal Statutes, Congressional Records, and Constitution

40 Stat. 1017 (1918).
56 Cong. Rec. 10761-65 (1918).
114 Cong. Rec. 11206, 14694 (1968).
132 Cong. Rec. S14,449 (daily ed., 1 October 1986).
132 Cong. Rec. S14,034 (daily ed., 27 September 1986).
H. Rep. No. 99-647, 99th Cong., 2nd Sess. (1986).
Pub. L. No. 73-652, §605, 48 Stat. 1103 (1934), now 47 U.S.C.A. 605 (1970).
Pub. L. No. 91-452, 84 Stat. 941 (1970).
Pub. L. No. 95-511, 92 Stat. 1783, codified at 50 U.S.C.S., §§1801–11 (1982 and Supp. III 1985).
Senate Report Number 541, 1986 U.S. Code Cong. and Admin. News 3580.
Senate Report Number 1097, 1968 U.S. Code Cong. and Admin. News 2178.
18 U.S.C.S., §§2020, 2510–20, 2522, 2707 (1968, 1986).
42 U.S.C.S., §1983 (1981).
U.S. Const., Amendment 4.

United States State Statutes and Constitutions

Alaska Const., Art. I, §1.
Alaska Stat., §42.20.310.
Ariz. Const., Art. II, §8.
Ariz. Rev. Stat. Ann., §§13-3005 (1), (2).
Cal. Const., Art. I, §1.
Cal. Penal Code, §§629.38, 632.5 (Supp.), 633.
Conn. Gen. Stat. Ann., §52-570 (d) (a) (1).
Fla. Const., Art. I, §§12, 23.
Haw. Const., Art. I, §§6–7.
Haw. Rev. Stat. Ann. §803-41 (Supp.).
Idaho Code, §18-6702 (2) (d), (e).
Ill. Const., Art. I, §6.
Ill. Rev. Stat. ch. 38, ¶ 108B-(1) (o).
Iowa Code Ann., §§727.8, 808 B.2 (2) (c).
Kan. Stat. Ann. §21-4001.
La. Const., Art. I, §5.
La. Rev. Stat. Ann., §14:322.1 (A), (D).
Me. Rev. Stat. Ann., title 15, §§709 (A) (B) (Supp.).

Mo. Rev. Stat., §542.400 (2) (3) (Supp.).
Mont. Const., Art. II, §10.
N.Y. Penal Law (see §§250.00, 250.05.).
Ohio Rev. Code Ann., §§2933.53 (B) (4) and (F) (3).
S.C. Const., Art. I, §10.
Utah Code Ann., §77-23A-4 (7) (a), (b), (8).
Wash. Const., Art. I, §7.
Wash. Rev. Code Ann., §9.73.030 (1) (a), (b), (2) (b) (Supp.).
W. Va. Code, §62-1D-3 (c) (2) (Supp.).

Canadian Statutes and Parliamentary Records

An Act to Incorporate the Bell Telephone Company of Canada (S.C. 1880, c. 67, §25).
The Alberta Government Telephones Act (R.S.A. 1970, c. 12, as amended).
Canadian Charter of Rights and Freedoms (Part I of the Constitution Act 1982 [Schedule B of the Canada Act 1982, U.K.), c. 11, §8).
Criminal Code (R.S.C. 1970, c. C-34, as amended, Part IV.I).
Criminal Law Amendment Act (1977, S.C. 1976–77, c. 53).
Crown Liability Act (R.S.C. c. C-38, as amended).
Interpretation Act (R.S.C. 1970, c. I-23).
Minutes and Proceedings of the Standing Committee on Justice and Legal Affairs (5 February 1970, 2nd session, 28th Parliament, No. 7:7).
Official Secrets Act (R.S.C. 1970, c. 0-3, as amended).
Privacy Act (1968 [B.C.], c. 39).
The Privacy Act (1970 [Man.], c. 74).
The Privacy Act, 1974 (1973–74 [Sask.], c. 80).
Protection of Privacy Act (1974, S.C. 1973–74, c. 50).
The Telephone Act (R.S.M. 1970, c. T 40, as amended by 1977 [Man.], c. 45).
The Telephone Act (R.S.O. 1970, c. 457).

PE 1702 .A5 no.79

Under cover of law